THE DIVORCE DECISION

THE DIVORCE DECISION

GARY RICHMOND

WORD PUBLISHING
Dallas · London · Sydney · Singapore

Library of Congress Cataloging-in-Publication Data

Richmond, Gary, 1944–
    The divorce decision : what it can mean for your children, your finances, your emotions, your relationships, your future / Gary Richmond.
        p.   cm.
    1. Divorce—United States. 2. Divorce—Religious aspects—Christianity. 3. Divorced people—United States—Psychology.
I. Title.
HQ834.R43   1988
306.8'9—dc19   88-18661
ISBN 0-8499-3104-5 (pbk.)   CIP

    1 2 3 9   9 8 7 6 5

Printed in the United States of America

To my beloved Single Parent Fellowship group who taught me what divorce was like and moved me to write this book. Especially to Dale Thompson, Rich Crosley and Steve Richmond, my brother, who let me look into every corner of their lives if it would help others.

A percentage of the author's royalties will be given to the First Evangelical Free Church of Fullerton to assist single-parent children.

Contents

Preface

THE INTERVIEW PROCESS that brought me to the First Evangelical Free Church of Fullerton was rigorous, draining, and perplexing because there was no way to prepare for it. It was the first time in history that someone was being offered the opportunity to serve as a full-time pastor to single parents and my experience had primarily been in youth work and Christian education. I had worked for seven years at the Los Angeles Zoo, and many who interviewed me theorized that that might be the exact type of preparation that would make me the ideal candidate for the position.

I didn't really know much about single-parents ministry, and dealing with people during the traumatic period of their divorces had not been the most common task in my twenty-two previous years of ministry. Carol and I had several very close friends who were divorced, and it was their experiences that created a desire to reach out to people going through that same dark passage. Churches, especially the evangelical church, had for too long turned their heads away from the divorced, treating them like second-class citizens or modern-day lepers. It was time to do more for them. Many were the helpless, innocent victims of their mate's adultery, abuse, and abandonment. Somebody needed to stand by them, encourage them, and help them get back into life. The First Evangelical Free Church had an active single-parents program that had been primarily developed by the single parents themselves. They had some pastoral help but had for the most part developed the program on their own. It was special and it was an empathetic family that reached out to its own wounded and nursed them back to health in a caring and protected environment. I really wanted to be a part of this already vital group.

I was asked every imaginable question during my interview, but there was one question that has come back to haunt me more than all the rest. That question was, "Gary, what do you think will be the most difficult aspect of caring for a single-parents group?" Never having done that, I was forced to guess. "I would think that daily dealing with people who are in great emotional trauma would take its toll on you."

My guess has turned out to be right. Yet what I now know is that the toll that it takes on me does not begin to compare with the toll it takes on them. After three years of viewing their hurt, I am compelled to write this book. I think you could call it an act of conscience. I have always felt that if someone is facing a great danger, they ought to be warned. I am my brother and sister's keeper. I think that is at the heart of ministry. If I were in danger, I would want to be warned, and so I will do unto others as I would have done unto me. I will warn them. I realize that some will not want to be warned, and once warned will still prefer risk to reason. But that will be their right and I will have played my part.

When the government forced the tobacco industry to indicate that smoking might be injurious to one's health, it became the individual's responsibility to decide. Many have since decided to quit, most have not. Both groups bear the consequences of their choices, and there will be consequences. Do you remember Harry Truman, the old man who lived on Mount Saint Helens? I remember him. He was characterized as a willful old codger used to doing things his way. He was warned that the mountain was going to blow, but he chose to stay, and he bore the consequences. The consequences were far more devastating than anyone could have reckoned. Harry was snuffed out in a second. He most likely didn't feel a thing, and dying on a mountain he loved . . . well, there are worse ways to go. The awesome blast of Mount Saint Helens was an event, but divorce is a process. Whether you initiate the process or are subjected to it, the outcome will ultimately be the same. You will hurt. You will hurt more than you have ever hurt before, and the process will never really end.

You may never experience closure even if you are now thirty and live to be sixty.

If you are trying to make the decision to divorce your mate, you are probably experiencing the greatest emotional pain of your life. People rarely make good decisions when they feel the way that you are feeling, so take the time to read this book. It has been developed to help you see the issues that you will face if you opt for divorce.

You might want to know what this book is about. It is about what happens to you after you divorce. It is all about aftereffects, and be sure there are many of them. I think I owe it to you to tell you what they are likely to be. The general misimpression is that a person will have a great chance to be happy if she/he dumps the bum or sends the witch away. Studies have proven that this is just not the case. The truth is that you will introduce a new chain of events into your life. If you had known how painful they would be, you would have stayed with the process of working at your marriage problems longer, maybe even until they were solved. If you divorce, you will open your own private Pandora's Box, and what comes out will come to haunt you in some way for the rest of your life. There are of course legitimate reasons to divorce, and those we will discuss in due time. But for now, let me stick to warning you of the consequences of divorce.

1. If you have children you will damage them in several ways if you opt for divorce. Children of divorce are more likely to commit suicide or become homosexual or promiscuous. They are more likely to

spend time in jail or be a behavioral problem in school. They will tend to be insecure. Most likely, they will lose the ability to believe the possibility that "they lived happily ever after." They will lose their trust for their parents. More and more they will take their cues from their peers. Because their peers base their lives on drugs, sex, and rock and roll, you may not find that desirable. Children of divorce experience more illness, both mental and physical, than do children whose parents stay together. They will be subjected to the repeated tuggings of two parents fighting for their time and emotional support, and they will usually be compelled to take sides, even though that is the last thing in the world that they would want to do.

No one can convince me that I have overstated the case with the children. I have seen these things daily, through the course of thousands of hours of counseling over the last twenty years. Even as a youth director it was clear that the most troubled group of teens that I dealt with were from broken or breaking homes.

2. If you choose to divorce, your finances will be affected for years to come. There is rarely enough to go around. The usual aftereffect is that both parties are assigned to a bare-bones existence.

3. If you choose to divorce with the thought that love is better the second time around, you need to know that second marriages have a less than 30 percent chance of surviving five years or more. A third marriage has less than 15 percent chance of survival. And as people add to the number of marriages, their chance of success continues to decline.

4. Don't think for a minute that your mate will be the only one fighting for what you feel is your fair share of the money. Wait until you see your own lawyer's bill. In California the average couple spends $15,000 fighting for children, lawn chairs, the dog, and the car. Lawyers are the only winners in a divorce proceeding.

5. Choosing to divorce means putting the major decisions of your life into the hands of a judge who may or may not be fair. You may be assigned a bad judge or a good judge, but it will be nothing more than the luck of the draw.

6. Divorcing your mate means divorcing your friends. If you go to church, it means facing the reality that your faith will not be respected as it once was. You will find yourself starting over in the making of friends, and you will feel awkward in the making of new ones. Old friends are best.

7. Divorce is a process that never really ends. When you first begin the process there is the hope that the other person will be out of your life. The reality is that you will probably see her/him a good deal more than you thought you would, and at the times that you would most hope not to. You will see them at your children's school activities such as concerts, games, and graduations. You will talk to them to arrange child visitation, discuss emergencies, deal with your children's discipline. You may be inquiring as to why support payments are late or even nonexistent. Their names will keep coming up, and you are sure to have some well-meaning friend address your new mate by your old mate's name. You will need

their signature for some piece of unfinished business. It just never ends. *Never!*

8. Most importantly, you will have to deal with your own conscience if you decide to divorce. You know that down deep you will answer to God on this issue, and by now I'm sure that you are aware that God has expressed Himself on this issue. He says in the Book of Malachi that He hates divorce and He tells us why. Broken promises and broken children are at the center of His deepest feelings on this subject.

It could be that you have a very legitimate case for divorce, and I would not want to be the one that kept you in an impossible situation that would destroy you or your children. But you need to know that being divorced is so devastating that you must face its consequences squarely as you make your decision. Fixing your marriage may be easier than breaking it, although at this moment you find that impossible to believe. In the chapters ahead you will be exposed to the thoughts just expressed in great depth. You owe it to yourself, your mate, your children, your family, your friends, and your God to explore this issue carefully.

You also need to know that there is hope and more than hope—help. So I encourage you to read on. I assure you that you are in for many surprises, some good, some bad, but all are necessary to know. God be with you during this search. Let Him walk through this valley of shadows with you, and you will be sure to find your way.

Introduction

IF YOU ARE TRYING TO DECIDE whether or not to divorce your mate, you are probably experiencing
the greatest emotional pain of your life. People rarely
make good decisions when they are feeling the way
you are feeling, so take the time to read this book,
chapter by chapter. You know the decision is an important one, and I can assure you this will affect the
rest of your life in ways you could never have imagined. You can't imagine these because you have never
been down this road before. I've been down this road
hundreds of times with others. Let me share their
experiences with you. It may help you to make the
right decision. It may be that divorcing your mate
will prove to be the best solution to the dilemma in
which you find yourself. On the other hand, it may be

that you are trading a painful but repairable relationship for Pandora's Box.

When ·making a decision of this magnitude, it is wise to count the cost. Important decisions are rarely made in isolation. The more important the decision, the more people there are involved. As painful as this may be to hear or think about, you must consider how your decision will affect others. If you choose divorce, you will forever alter the course of your children's lives. The way you relate to your closest friends will never be the same. Your immediate family will be affected forever. There are very few smooth, clean divorces, so you can almost be assured that you will find yourself at the mercy of a judge who may or may not find the time to review your case thoroughly and lawyers who will charge their exorbitant fees whether or not they had time to prepare for your case. What I am saying is that you will be handing some of the most important decisions of your life into someone else's hands. And that someone else is most likely sick and tired of people not getting along.

Your finances will be immediately affected and your living standard will surely go down. There is never enough to go around.

I haven't even mentioned the three big considerations.

1. How will you feel about yourself if you leave your mate?
2. Can you know with any assurance that your future will be better than it is now?
3. How does God view your decision?

I assure you, there are answers to all of these questions and many not here mentioned. Read on—you owe it to yourself to know the issues involved with this important decision.

Not too many years ago Kenny Rogers sang a song called "The Gambler." I wept when I heard it for the first time because many of the words in the song were words of wisdom that my father had taught me just before he died. He died when I was fifteen.

During my childhood, Friday night was poker night. My father would invite a few good friends over. No one was allowed to lose more than ten dollars, and if they did, they became the dealer. By age twelve I was begging my way into the weekly game and managed to lose my fifty-cent weekly allowance with incredible regularity. My father never once bailed me out, nor would he let any of his friends come to my rescue. He would, on Saturday, however, remind me of the most important principles of the game: knowing when to hold them . . . knowing when to fold them . . . knowing when to walk away . . . and knowing when to run.

That's what this book is all about. Holding them or folding them. This may be the most important decision left in your life. May God help you play your cards right.

1

The Children

IF YOU HAVE CHILDREN of any age, they will be affected in an adverse manner by a divorce. To varying degrees, to be sure, but they will be affected. You owe it to your children to consider them in your choice.

Children have a dream to which they are entitled—at least in childhood. This dream we call "And they lived happily ever after." It has everything to do with how they view their future. If they gain the view that their future is uncertain and unpredictable, their lives will manifest several disastrous symptoms.

As you read the following story, you will begin to see the implications of your choice more clearly.

I'D THROW THE FLOWERS HIGHER

Brandie and Stephen are children of divorce. On the outside, nothing is apparently different about them. They are both attractive, well-groomed, and extremely active children. Stephen is nine, handsome like his father, and tan, as is typical for a California boy. Brandie is eight. She is blonde, sandy blonde, I would say, and has a generous number of freckles cascading down both sides of her cute pug nose. Brandie is refreshingly outspoken. When I met her for the first time in the waiting room at church she sized me up and said, "I can tell already I'm going to be bored."

I laughed and said, "Don't be so sure, Brandie. I used to work at a zoo and I have pictures all over my wall of the animals I used to take care of." Her blue eyes opened a bit wider, she shrugged and followed me down the hallway, as did her father and brother.

Dave had brought his children in because he knew something was bothering them, but they wouldn't tell him what it was. As most fathers, Dave was awarded custody for Friday, Saturday, and Sunday on every other weekend. The weekends were usually full of free communication, but for reasons unknown to Dave, his children seemed a bit depressed and subdued. Brandie would hardly talk to him at all.

When we sat down in my office, Brandie walked to my string bass that was standing in the corner. I could tell she was impressed with its size and more impressed when she plucked it. Her father was slightly uncomfortable with what she was doing, but I was very glad she was beginning to feel free in the office.

After we began to talk, it became clear that the children were not going to talk freely in front of their dad. I asked Dave if he would step out to the reception area so I might talk to the children alone.

I knew that I might only get one opportunity to see them, so I tried to move as quickly to the problem as possible.

"It really hurts when your parents get a divorce, doesn't it?" I said quietly.

Stephen frowned and nodded his head in hardy agreement. Brandie's reply surprised me.

"It's not so bad. Didn't bother me. You just get more moms and more dads. It's no big deal."

Stephen frowned and blurted out, "You're not telling the truth, Brandie. It hurt you a lot."

"Is that true, Brandie, did it hurt you a lot?" I asked.

"Yes," she said with her head bowed. "It would make me cry if I thought about it. So whenever I do, I take my thoughts to my secret place and lock them up. Then I don't have to think about it anymore. Then I don't have to cry."

"Have you put a lot of those thoughts in your secret place, Brandie?" I asked.

She looked up with sad eyes and nodded yes. Just for a second I wondered if she would begin to cry. She didn't though, and I wondered if she had just made a quick trip to her secret place.

I thought a minute and inquired, "Is your secret place getting full?" She nodded and softly said, "Yes."

"What will you do when it gets full, Brandie?"

She didn't answer, and I felt moved to say to

Brandie that crying was God's way of letting our problems out so they could go away.

I could tell Brandie was getting a little uncomfortable, and I let her change the subject.

"I don't say the F-word anymore," she said.

I swallowed, took a deep breath, and then probed, "What word is that?"

"F-A-M-I-L-Y," she replied.

"Family?!" I exclaimed with both relief and surprise.

"'Gang' is the new word. People just come and go from a gang, and that's just the way it is. It's no big deal. It doesn't hurt."

"Do you dream a lot about your real mom and dad getting married again?" I asked.

Stephen and Brandie both nodded, and Stephen said, "Mom's going to get married to a new man. We don't like him very much. He's too bossy."

"What does he tell you to do?"

"He tells us what to eat for breakfast, just like he thinks he's our real dad."

"Is he over for breakfast a lot?" I asked.

"Just when he's too tired to go home at night."

"Is this what's been making you so sad that your mom is going to get married again, but not to your real dad?"

They both nodded yes.

"But there is one good thing that's going to happen," said Brandie. "What's that?" I asked.

"I'm going to be the flower girl for my mom's wedding."

"That sounds like fun," I said.

"You know what? If my mom would marry my real dad again, I would throw the flowers higher."

Brandie went on while Stephen nodded occasionally to affirm his younger sister's assessment of their future.

"You know what, Pastor Gary? My mom doesn't yell at the new man yet. But she will. And you know what?"

"What, Brandie?" I asked, wondering what she would surprise me with this time.

"She's going to start yelling at the new man, and he won't like it much and they'll get divorced. Then she'll get married to my real dad again." She smiled, sat back fully in her chair, cocked her head, folded her arms, and said, "Then everything will be all right again." She nodded her head again to show that was all she had to say.

You and I know that everything will not be all right again. In fact, there is a 70 percent chance that Brandie's mother will divorce again in five years. That means that they are likely to face the trauma once again. They will view the deterioration, feel the tension, and experience the fear of change, too much change, too early in their lives.

Butch is twelve years old. We recently used him on a panel of children who were asked various questions about what it was like to go through a divorce. The specific question that Butch's answer stunned the audience with was, "What feelings did you have when you learned that your parents were going to get a divorce?"

Butch is a bundle of energy and a little sensitive to be answering in front of three hundred adults. His father was in the audience also. He looked down, stammered a little, and finally blurted out, "I would lie in bed and listen to my parents argue, and then my heart would beat twice as fast as usual because I just knew one of them would come in and tell me that they were going to get a divorce." Butch glanced quickly at his father and then looked down at the table. The audience was absolutely silent as they considered his answer. I could see in their eyes that they were wondering if their children had stayed awake with hearts pounding. Each parent considered to what extent their children felt anguished over the breakup of their families. I found myself teary, feeling for Butch and feeling for this group of parents. I wondered about the wisdom of having asked this question in front of a group of people who couldn't change the past and hoped that in some way it might impact the future.

I Don't Know If Anyone Loves Me Anymore

Recently a father shared a very personal moment he had experienced with his five-year-old daughter. The situation was that the marriage had been deteriorating significantly for more than five years. His daughter, Julie, had witnessed either harsh or no communication throughout her brief life.

Her parents were not staying together in the same bedroom. The intensity of the fighting had been accelerating, and Bob would simply leave the house rather than stay and be berated in front of the children. Sharon, his wife, would fall into depression and sit for hours doing needlepoint or reading the same page of the newspaper over and over again. The two youngest children were then left to more or less fend for themselves. Their diet had become one of cold cereal or quick snacks to tide them over until mealtimes (if there were mealtimes).

At 9:30 one night, Bob heard Julie quietly call out to him as he was walking to his own bedroom through their extensive hallway. He stuck his head into her room and gruffly asked, "What are you doing up?"

Julie reached up her arms and whispered softly, "Daddy, will you hold me?" Her voice was cracking and her eyes were moist in the corners. Bob pulled her close, and she said, her voice quivering with emotion, "Daddy, it's just that I don't know if anyone loves me anymore." Bob held her in his arms until she fell asleep, but before she did, he repeated over and over again, "Julie, I love you, and I always will."

I want to stop periodically and underline some specific points of consideration for you as you move through this book.

1. Divorce will leave your child with the inner feeling that his or her world is uncertain and unpredictable. (This has many implications that we will discuss in other chapters.)

2. Divorce robs children of their fondest hope;

namely, "And they lived happily ever after." Since they never really let go of this fantasy, it leads them through a series of disappointments.

3. The process of divorce, and it is a process not an event, produces a steady chain of excruciatingly painful events for children.

4. Because the parents are feeling such traumatic and dramatic pain, they are often without the ability to help others, even their own children. This of course leaves children wondering if anybody loves them during the same period that their parents are suffering.

Tammy, in the next story, illustrates one of the tragic perceptions that children entertain. They perceive that somehow the divorce or separation was their fault. This is true about the vast majority of children, not only those I have talked to. Studies clearly show that this is a common perception. Rich Buehler, the well-known radio host of "Talk from the Heart," shared a fact concerning all victims recently. He told us, "All of us, especially children, think superstitiously. We believe that good things happen to good people and bad things happen to bad people." This is true and the more traumatic the event the more negative feelings children will have about themselves. Divorce is extremely traumatic, so divorced children are very subject to thinking they are worthless, hopeless, and being punished. They think this couldn't happen to good children. Rich called to mind the wonderful scene in *The Sound of Music* where Baron von Trapp proposed to Maria. She said yes, and then do you remember what Maria sang? "Somewhere in my wicked childhood I must have done something good." Now read Tammy's story with this in mind.

I'LL BE GOOD MOMMY

Todd's wife had been gone five weeks. He had begged her not to go. He knew that they had lots of troubles, but probably not any more than anybody else. Todd had never felt this alone before. Had it not been for his four-year-old son and six-year-old daughter, he was sure that he would have taken his life. For them, he must be strong. They needed him more than they would ever need anybody again in their lives, and there was no way that he would let them down. His wife Sherry had let the kids down, too. They wondered what they had done that was so bad that mommy didn't want to be with them anymore. For several nights Todd had rocked them to sleep as they quietly sobbed in his arms.

Sherry seemed desperate the night she left. She had managed to blurt out that getting married had been a big mistake. She had told him that she had never really loved him, but she married him just to get away from her parents. Her parting words were, "Todd, I've got to get away for a while. I have another chance to be happy and I'm just not going to miss it." She glanced at the children and Todd noticed a mixture of pain and guilt. She turned away and walked out the door. "I'll call you when I'm ready to talk," she said coldly.

She hadn't called. Tammy's teacher had called though, wanting to know what was going on at home to make Tammy so unhappy at school. Todd was embarrassed, but he explained to the teacher that Tammy's mother had left and he didn't have any idea where she was. He wondered what the teacher was really thinking. Maybe she was thinking he had been a terrible husband or something like that. She seemed nice enough though and promised to give Tammy some special attention.

Todd's most painful moment came the day after the teacher's phone call. He picked up Tammy from school, and she proudly showed him her drawing. It was clearly a house with four stick figures in front of it: a mommy, a daddy, a brother, and a sister. Todd felt a twinge of pain. That was what he wanted their family to look like too.

"That's nice, Tammy. You are really a good artist." Tammy looked at her drawing and nodded in agreement. She laid it in her lap gently and stared at it all the way home.

When she got home, she ran into her parents' bedroom. After several minutes, Todd wondered what she was doing in there. He stepped softly to his bedroom door and his heart broke just a little bit more because of what he saw. Tammy was holding her drawing up to a picture of her mother and telling it all about the drawing and her day.

"Mommy, this is what I drew today. This is what I want our family to look like. This family is happy. We could be happy again Mommy. I'll be good if you come home. I miss you Mommy."

Can you feel Tammy's hurt? Isn't it clear that she believes her mommy left because she had been bad? Tammy will spend years feeling that she is a bad girl because she feels that good things happen to good people and bad things happen to bad people.

I think you are getting the picture that divorce is a very devastating event in the lives of children. The following two poems were written by different girls, one ten and one fifteen. The first we found in Mary Griffin's "A Cry for Help." It was written by a ten-year-old being treated for depression. These poems speak for themselves. They are eloquent expressions of the emotional chaos children are forced to endure.

> Divorce shakes you off the ground.
> Divorce whirls you all around.
> Divorce makes you all confused.
> Divorce forces you to choose.
> Divorce makes you feel all sad.
> Divorce pushes you to be mad.
> Divorce makes you wonder who cares.
> Divorce leaves you thoroughly scared.
> Divorce makes a silent home.
> Divorce leaves you all alone.
> Divorce is supposed to be the answer.
> Divorce, in fact, is emotional cancer.

The following poem was written by Jeni Goodloe when she was fifteen. She is lovely, the all-American girl, well grounded in her faith. Her poem was written in the midst of the reality of divorce.

Life

I had lost all my happiness,
All my joy;
My world was turned upside down.

I had to get out—
Get out and think things through.
I walked a mile or maybe two.
It wasn't long 'till I came upon some yellow daffodils.
Why so beautiful?
I asked myself.
Bright green grass,
Shining rays of sun;
All so comforting.
But then clouds started forming,
And rain began pouring,
The beauty was more beautiful than ever.
For now I knew what made the daffodils
The green grass so beautiful.
If there was no rain to make them grow
There'd be no daffodils to show.
So as with life; if there were no
Unhappiness to make us grow
There'd be no happiness to show.

These two poems clearly demonstrate children working through the pain of a divorce. It is often as painful for children as for adults, and the effects are of a considerably longer and deeper duration.

A remarkable article ran recently in the *Orange County Register*. It was entitled, "Ties That Bind: Divorce and Teen Suicide," by Bryce Christiansen.

The article states that adolescent suicide rates have risen 300 percent during the last thirty years. This statistic had a remarkable correlation to the rise in the divorce rate during the same period. In fact, the

American divorce rate has doubled since 1960, the article states. It would be impossible to separate the implications. The children of divorce are much more likely to take their own lives than children whose parents have stayed together.

Bryce states, "Once parents in an unhappy marriage stayed together, for the children, but now more than two-thirds of those seeking divorce have children at home."

Suicide is not the only problem that escalates because of divorce. Children who have experienced a divorce are absent from school at much higher rates than those who have not. They get lower grades and are much more likely to be discipline problems. Why? After most divorces, both parents must work. The children are mostly latch-key "orphans" from about eleven years on.

We have long quoted the saying, "The idle brain is the devil's playground." Latch-key children have far too much unsupervised time. As all humans, they will, if left uncontrolled, be likely to do what they can do instead of what they should do.

It is fascinating to follow the performance of children in school as they are taken through a divorce. Their report cards act as an emotional barometer. I had heard that this was the case but needed to see it for myself before I was willing to put it in print. I asked a close friend if he could send me copies of his son's report cards. I wanted the report cards the year before his son became aware of the divorce, during the divorce, and the year after the divorce. They bore out the statements concerning the report cards being an emotional indicator.

Tommy was in the second grade during 1984–85. His parents were in counseling, but Tommy didn't know that. For all he knew, he was in the average American family. They went on vacations together, helped him with his homework, ate fast foods, and watched television. They attended church most Sundays and visited his grandparents with regularity. Tommy was oblivious to his parents' problems.

During 1985–86 Tommy was in third grade. His mother had filed for divorce, and his parents separated. An awesome custody battle ensued. Tommy was emotionally distraught. He wanted most to be with his father but didn't want his mother to think that he didn't love her. It was a hard year.

In 1986–87 Tommy entered the fourth grade. The court battles raged on, and he was examined by a psychologist to see with which parent he would live. He was shifted from home to home and was exposed to his parents' anger and depression. Life didn't mean as much to him any more.

Compare the report cards and the comments. See if the effects of divorce are obvious.

Tommy's Report Cards

	Pre-divorce 1984–85	Separation 1985–86	Divorce Continues 1986–87
Reading	B+	C+	C
Mathematics	B+	B–	C–
Spelling	A	B	C+
Effort/Citizenship	Outstanding	Satisfactory	Needs Improvement

There were no teacher's comments in 1984–85. Comments in 1985–86 included the following, "Tommy is bright but doesn't work up to his capacity. He seems nervous and distracted. Tommy's work is inconsistent." In 1986–87 there was a drastic drop in Tommy's study habits, and the teacher mentioned that she wished he would make better use of his time.

Tommy's report cards began to improve in 1988, but he still shows evidence of a good deal of insecurity. In the fifth grade Tommy improved in most ways but showed an inordinate fear of being left alone and does not sleep well unless he can share a room with another person.

I interviewed a group of teachers from my son's elementary school and asked them if they could see visible or dramatic changes in behavior when a child was being taken through a divorce. The reaction was in itself dramatic and visible. Among the thoughts most often expressed were, "They look like zombies, staring out into space completely unable to concentrate." They often become rebellious or perform negative behavior to gain badly needed attention. They withdraw ashamed and embarrassed because they aren't living with both parents.

Statistics show a dramatic rise in drug usage in this group. One of the most dramatic moments of my ministry occurred in this context. I was called to St. Jude Hospital in Fullerton where one of the parents in our Single Parents Fellowship was watching her son fight for his life. He had contracted gangrene from a dirty needle while taking cocaine. Afraid to get help and expose his problem, he tried to treat himself and the gangrene got a roaring head start on the doctors. The infection had spread up his arm and down his back and the method of treatment was painful beyond imagination. In addition to intravenous and antibiotics, they performed daily surgery making long incisions so they might reach under the skin and scrape the infection off the muscle. They left the incisions open to drain and to be scraped daily. I can imagine no treatment more painful.

As the days passed, the doctors had expressed some concern that they would be able to stop the infection before it claimed this young man's life. Although they were divorced, both parents stayed at his bedside to support him. There was a great deal of tension in the room because the mother had been forced to take her former husband back to court for a large amount of back child support. While their son was dealing with the possibility of his own death, the parents finally tangled over their financial problems. The phone rang. It was their son's best friend. He was calling to say that the drug dealer wanted his money, and he wanted it soon. If he didn't get it soon, he was going to do a little damage to the mother's home. Can you imagine the pressure on all the members of the family, especially the son, at that moment?

The son survived and seems to be making the adjustment to a responsible lifestyle after several confused years.

The unsupervised lifestyle of the divorced child leads to a predisposition to chemical dependencies.

They lean more heavily on their peer group for their values, and if you haven't noticed lately their peer groups are not a sufficient foundation for a value system. The current basis for the value system of the teen culture is drugs, sex, and rock and roll. If children don't get their values from their parents, they will get them from their peers. And that is rarely good news.

Promiscuous behavior is likely if teens are left alone. They need to be loved, and if they are not they will try to find love somewhere. They will be willing to experiment to achieve intimacy.

In many cases divorce predisposes children to homosexuality. It is now considered a fact that children establish their sexual identity between the ages of two to six years. They do that by watching their parents. When one parent is removed from the home, the one sexual presence is elevated and emulated. Values are developed during this period also, and parents are their children's primary source of values. So, for whatever reason, children are at a distinct disadvantage if they are raised by only one parent.

I THINK YOU'RE RAISING A QUEER

Robby is now forty-one years of age and scared to death. Robby is dying of AIDS. His disease is in its early stages, and most of the time he ignores it. Yet in the soft, quiet moments, his alone time, he is afraid to the very center of his being.

He contracted his disease from Merlin. Merlin was a pilot for a major airline. He died several months ago. He and Robby were homosexual lovers and had been so for a long time. Both were very promiscuous outside their own relationship. They played a type of Russian roulette and pulled the trigger one too many times.

The Robbys and the Merlins are often shaped by the major events of their lives. They are responsible for their choices to be sure, nevertheless, events may have predisposed them to bad choices. They will be held responsible for their choices, but so will the others who helped them make them.

Robby's mother was Barbara. She married very young at eighteen in reaction to a brutal and abusive childhood. Barbara's mother would often ask her questions like, "What rock did you just crawl out from under?" She blamed Barbara over and over for being a millstone in her life and blamed her for every failure. Barbara was conceived before her parents were married, and her mother married for honor, not love. Barbara's mother divorced her husband three years later because she could no longer tolerate the beatings she received or his degrading alcoholism. Barbara was always a reminder of a bad choice, and her mother never let her forget it.

Her mother didn't remarry for ten years, which left Barbara without a male influence during the critical years when sexual identity is established. Barbara only remembers seeing her real father five times in her life.

Barbara also married an abuser who was alcoholic. Within two and a half years she was divorced. Even before they separated, he never stayed home and their son Robby was never exposed to a positive male role model during his childhood. Barbara was the only present factor in his young life.

Barbara's Aunt Rose was a crude, blunt, but honest individual. She looked Barbara in the eye one day and said, "Barbara, I think you're raising a queer. Robby never plays with little boys, he's always wearing your clothes, and he wants to be the princess in the school play."

Barbara didn't know what to think because people didn't deal with homosexuality thirty-five years ago. She had no idea what to say or what to do.

By nine years of age, Robby was seeing a child psychologist for social maladjustment. He was a loner. The other children made fun of him and teased him mercilessly. During this period his younger sister, Beth, became very ill and received by far the most attention and affection from Barbara.

Barbara remarried when Robby was thirteen. The man she married turned out to be far worse than the first man she married. He had walked away from his first marriage when his own son was three. When his wife died, he was forced to take custody of his son. Billy was now fifteen and had also been raised without the influence of a male for all those years. Billy joined Robby as a stepbrother, which turned out to be the turning point for Robby. Billy was already acting out his homosexuality, and he introduced Robby to acting out his homosexuality.

From that time on, Robby considered himself a

homosexual although he consistently practiced bi-
sexuality.

Billy, the stepbrother, was a bisexual and deserted
three wives and several children during his pitiful
lifetime. What a mess.

Robby had been practicing his homosexuality for
years, but it was never confirmed to Barbara until
her son was discharged from the Navy for homosexual panic. He thought the Navy had told his mother,
but they hadn't. As she listened to his story, she was
stunned. Aunt Rose was right, she had been raising a
queer.

Barbara has for years lived under a strained relationship with Robby. Since his high school years, he
has made it clear that he cannot stand her. He has
taken delight in her humiliation and flaunts his homosexuality whenever he can. During a candid moment,
he shared in despair, "Mother, I don't even know who
I am."

Robby will most likely be dead by the time this
material is published. It seems clear to me that his
destiny was written in part by a process—Divorce.

Without a long explanation, let me suggest three
other effects of divorce on children.

1. Children of divorce will be much more likely to
   spend time in jail.
2. They will experience more health problems,
   both mental and physical.
3. They will have much greater risk that their marriages will fail.

I don't know just what turn of events took place that made people think that their happiness and well-being was more important than that of their children, but at minimum I hope you are becoming aware of the disastrous effect of divorce on children. Two-thirds of the people making the divorce decision have children.

2

The Finances
of Divorce

I HATE BEING A DIVORCE LAWYER," said Dean. "And
I'm not going to be one much longer. I'm going
back to criminal law." His pin-striped suit needed a
trip to the cleaners, and he could have used a little
sprucing up, a haircut, and a shave. He was wearing
the badge of someone who just didn't give a rip about
anything.

"Why criminal law over divorce law?" I inquired.

"Everyone is out to get everyone. No one is ever
satisfied. Kids are getting the shaft and everyone
is lying about everything. They are lying through
their teeth and everyone's angry at someone all the
time."

"What angers people the most?" I asked. His answer surprised me. "There is never enough money to

go around. Everyone thinks they are going to maintain the same standard of living, and when they don't
it really burns them. They resent paying my bill, and I
feel like I'm ripping off poor people who I helped
make poor."

"What makes criminal law any better?" I asked. "It
seems to me that you would be dealing with some
pretty scuzzy characters and that helping them get off
would leave you wondering what you had really accomplished."

"Yes that's true, but they know they are scuzzy characters and they are thankful for whatever you can do
for them. I'm defending a gang leader from down-
town east L.A. His gang calls him 'Green Eyes.' I'm
sure he's killed people. He's being tried for armed
robbery. It looks like I'm going to get him off with a
light sentence because he's cooperating with the po-
lice on a case involving another gang in the area. He
treats me like his best friend, and his family is always
doing nice things for me. It's just nice dealing in a
situation where there isn't so much anger."

After spending time as a single parent pastor, I
understand Dean's feelings. There is never enough
money to go around.

It has been a not-so-unusual occurrence to find
people living in their cars following their divorces.
On one occasion we met a mother who had spent a
week in her car with her two children. These two
darling little girls were resilient, to say the least. That
situation doesn't usually last too long—but it is more
common than you might think.

One of the men in our single parents group lived in

his car for more than a year. His circumstances were in part financial and partly self-imposed. He was using most of what he earned to retire debts he had accumulated during his marriage and the rest to pay spousal support. He developed an interesting lifestyle to reduce spending. Showering and shaving were accomplished at Cal State University at Fullerton. He carried a basketball and an athletic bag into the men's gym, giving the illusion that he was a student on his way to a physical education class. Nobody ever questioned him, even though this is the way he began most of the days of his life during that year.

Most of his food was obtained in local bars during "Happy Hour." Our man would order a coke and load up his plate with cheese, crackers, and whatever bill of fare they were serving. He told me jokingly that he actually gained a little weight on this diet. He ate out occasionally, but for the most part he was surviving just as I have described. He was offered housing on two occasions that I remember, but declined. Either he was too proud to receive help or he was punishing himself for failing in his marriage. He has since moved into conventional housing and is finally able to retain employment for prolonged periods. Of course these situations are extreme, but they're not all that uncommon.

Let me give you a feel for the average situation. John and Marsha had been married for thirteen years. Neither John nor Marsha remembered any of the years as happy years. They had two children early during their marriage. These were boys whom they both loved, and (for the most part) it was the boys for whom they lived. Marsha rarely worked during the marriage, but that was all right because John was an excellent provider and was inclined to try to win her much-needed affection by letting her do anything she wanted. John was not only an excellent provider, but he was also an excellent money manager.

During the thirteen years they accumulated three properties and John supplemented his $50,000-a-year income with professional photography, book sales, and raising rare birds for sale. There was never much in the bank in the way of savings, but the bills were always paid on time, and Marsha was inclined to spend any excess they had at the end of the month. They were rising on the equity of their properties and dreaming of the day that John could manage his own business. At least that was John's dream, because Marsha decided she wanted out.

She started her steady journey out of the marriage through the doors of a secular marriage and family counselor. For two years they went weekly at a cost of $60 per week. After satisfying a deductible of $400, they were charged $30 weekly because the insurance plan paid 50 percent. Two years and $3,500 later, the marriage counselor recommended divorce because she had run out of ideas. In a last ditch effort to save the marriage they sought a more expensive counselor who charged $100 an hour. Six months and $1,720 later, Marsha decided that it was time to bail out. So, as you can see, two and a half hears later, after spending $5,220 out of pocket on counseling, all John had to show for it were divorce papers and a broken heart. This was just the beginning.

Marsha demonstrated in her first legal action that she was out for blood. She asked for—and got—$1,200 a month, forcing John to borrow $900 monthly for child and spousal support. Because he wanted the children at least 50 percent of the time, a lengthy custody battle followed. During the battle it was necessary that John not miss or be late on any payment, so John found source after source to help him meet his monthly obligations. Marsha, knowing she was enjoying quite a nice financial advantage, prolonged the divorce proceedings through twenty-two delays.

She moved to a very nice condominium and was not working most of the time. She did go back to school and substitute taught occasionally. She took the summers off and made no effort to work at all, probably at the advice of her lawyer. All in all, she was able to stall long enough to obtain her teaching credentials, but during the entire divorce proceedings she never sought or obtained full-time employment. Through the time the divorce unfolded she complained she was not living up to the standard to which she was accustomed. She fought for more and more.

When they began the battle they enjoyed assets of about $75,000. Two and a half years later she was only to realize a total of $14,000. Greed had done her in. John obtained 57 percent of the custody time and was only to pay $200 monthly. That was a good final settlement for him, but at what cost? He began the process as a man with a family and $75,000 in assets. He became a man who sees his boys a little more than half the time and owes $30,000 to his lawyer and friends. At forty-four years of age and experiencing significant health problems, it will be a battle for him to turn his financial problems around. Recently John lost his job. He is trusting God with his life, but he still wonders when the trials will end.

Many of our single parents had comments to make about two questions we asked on a single parent survey. The comments below relate to one of these two questions: How did your standard of living change after your divorce? What was the worst financial problem you faced during the divorce?

1. A woman with two grown children said, "I had to move from a spacious four-bedroom, three-bath home to a small single room in the back of a friend's garage."
2. "We had to move from our own home into an apartment. We had to give up our two wonderful family dogs. There was neither room for them nor could we afford to feed them. This was especially hard on my son. He was an only child and loved the dogs very much."
3. "My divorce took me from comfort to poverty. I guess it's poverty when you can no longer pay your basic living expenses and you lose all your credit."
4. A young mother with three very young children said, "It seemed that most of the support that I received from my husband had to be used for child-care expenses so I could work. I don't make that much an hour so things are always tight. I go from day to day praying

nothing will break because I can't afford to fix it if it did. The thought of my car breaking down is terrifying. I feel stressed out just thinking about it."

5. "Bankruptcy!"

6. "I had to live on $700 a month for two years following my divorce. That was my salary. My husband never paid any child support for our son. Things were pretty hard for those first two years."

7. "I think the hardest part for me was that I could never afford to give my children any of the luxuries that their close friends enjoyed."

8. "I was left with all the bills because my husband was out of work. I couldn't pay the bills and care for three children so I was forced to go on welfare. I never thought it would happen to me."

9. "I had to file Chapter 13. My husband paid no support for the first year, I was laid off my job and my babysitter quit—everything fell apart."

10. "I lost half of my retirement. I am wondering about my future. It isn't that far away now."

11. "I was forced to take help from my own parents and my daughter for awhile. It was hard to leave our home and move to a rental house. We had to take in boarders to make ends meet."

12. "I couldn't afford car insurance for eleven months." [This is true for many of our single parents.]

13. "I moved from the middle class to welfare level. I hate not being able to pay the bills."

14. "I had to move back in with my parents. I have three little girls ages six, three, and two."
15. "We lost everything to the divorce."
16. "It's been hard since the divorce. You could best describe our life as, 'No frills.'"

"No frills," is a good description of life after divorce. There are exceptions, but no frills is the rule. During the three years that I have served as pastor to single parents there has rarely been a week that we have not been given the opportunity to reach out to a single person who has hit the financial wall.

Recently, I spent time with a courageous woman in our group who had come back financially from a sticky divorce situation. She had opened a dog grooming business alone and even lived in the back of it to save money. She had just broken even when the Whittier earthquake in California claimed her building. She is digging in once again to reopen her shop in another area, but as always since the divorce she is one step ahead of the bill collectors. Life had been hard and her greatest test is to trust from day to day that her most basic needs will be met.

I have spent countless hours with divorced mothers as they spread their bills out on my desk and say, "What am I going to do, pastor?" They bury their heads in their trembling hands and weep softly wondering how they are going to be able to feed their children and pay their rent or the water bill. I have met with several people who go without house gas or electricity because to them it is a luxury. Dental care is out of the question, and the only time they see a doctor is if they have an emergency. Car insurance isn't even considered by many. They aren't worried about a lawsuit. What could anybody take from them that hasn't already been taken by their mate or their lawyer?

What do you say to a woman with three young children who is making $5 an hour? She's living in a $500-a-month, two-bedroom apartment, and her husband (or rather, ex-husband who has moved out of state with his girlfriend) isn't sending his $400-a-month child-support payment any more. Her take-home paycheck is $670.

With rent at $500 (cheap for California), child care at $200, food at $250 (if she is clever), electricity at $30, house gas $25, phone $30, and water and trash $25, her budget is $1,030 a month. Even if her ex-husband sent the child support, she would have $40 to cover any auto repair, medical expenses, clothing for her and the children, entertainment of any kind, birthday gifts or cards, and car insurance. We haven't mentioned postage, appliance repair, or car gas or bus fare. If she works an additional part-time job, her income is diminished by child care. It just isn't worth it.

What would you tell her? I haven't thought of anything terribly clever yet, and most of the situations I hear about are salted with unpaid doctor bills, late car payments, nasty letters from collection agencies, and threatening letters from credit card institutions who are extended to their limits.

Financial life after divorce is the pits. If you don't believe me, ask around. Your divorced friends will verify everything that I have written.

3

The Legal System:
Blind Justice

ONE OF THE MOST FRIGHTENING ASPECTS of divorce is your encounter with the legal system. You will need a lawyer, and that, as you will see, is not good news. As with any of the professions, there are lawyers and then there are lawyers. I have asked several lawyers to comment on their feelings concerning divorce lawyers, and their comments were very entertaining. A friend who practices tax law referred to divorce lawyers as the "armpit of the profession." Another described them this way: "A divorce lawyer is to the legal profession what a proctologist is to the medical profession." He posed a fair question, "Who would want to practice that kind of law?"

Yet another respected and successful lawyer described his colleagues who practiced divorce law as "the dregs of the profession." He elaborated, "Divorce law is no fun. It's not as cut and dried as other forms of law. It is not as much a matter of skill as luck. Judges are very arbitrary in their rulings and the outcome may be entirely based on what they had for breakfast and how it's being digested. You see angry people, devastated children, saddened parents, and you are rarely finished with these cases. They can linger on for years because so many of your clients are vindictive."

These feelings about divorce lawyers are consistent among other members of their profession. The general consensus is that for the most part a lawyer who practices family law (divorce law) is either just starting out and is handed the cases that no one else will take, or they cannot make it doing any other kind of legal practice. The question remains, "Who would want to spend their waking hours helping families to dissolve?"

One of my own practices is to go occasionally with our single parents to their divorce trials so they won't have to be alone. Never is anybody more alone than when they are sitting in a courtroom being rejected by the person in this world who knows them best. Everything I have seen verifies what my three lawyer friends had told me. It is my opinion that the ratio of competent family law lawyers couldn't possibly be more than one good one for every nine bad ones. My opinions are borne out by the feelings expressed in our single parent survey.

Our survey gave them the opportunity to indicate the best description of their experience with the legal system. The words most often used were: "unscrupulous," "unprepared," "uncaring," "disorganized," "expensive," and "capricious." One of the most respected women in our group wrote, "I had a Christian lawyer who came recommended, but he never seemed to be aware of my case. I felt he was not well prepared. I felt that I was at his mercy. I also felt he did a very poor job."

The likelihood that you will turn the most important areas of your life over to the kind of professional that I have just described is very high. We are talking about the lives of your children and the disposition of your possessions. Very few of the divorces that I have witnessed have been clean or easy. The average divorce in our group cost $9,000. Many ran over $20,000, some $30,000, and the most expensive to date cost $55,000. The California Bar estimated that divorces which include child custody average $30,000. There is no good reason why they should be so expensive, except that it only takes one angry person to run up the bill to punish the other person. When you get two angry people, there is no telling what can happen. Let me share this story to illustrate how out of hand things can get.

Several months ago, George came to me seeking counsel. His wife of three years had decided that she no longer wanted to continue the relationship. This was George's first marriage and her second. George had come to the United States from an eastern country in which he had been a hero, a sports figure of much renown. There is no doubt cultural differences played a roll in the downfall of the relationship. In his culture, women feel a strong commitment to allow their men to provide direction for their homes. But George married a strong-willed, liberated American woman who was not about to give up an ounce of her independence to anybody. She had older children of her own, and even they received preferential treatment. George came last. You can imagine what a blow to his pride this was, and it was clear that he was both profoundly angry and deeply hurt. She was leaving him no opening for reconciliation and had, in fact, filed for divorce.

He asked me, "Where do I go from here, pastor?"

I said, "George, I think you need to see a lawyer so that he can explain your rights to you and protect your interests so she doesn't take advantage of you."

"I don't know any lawyers," he said. "Could you help me pick one?"

"I think so. Let me ask you some questions. If your case is simple, you can get a lawyer just starting out and save a lot of money. Do you own a home together or do you rent?"

"Rent."

"Do you have any assets that you have obtained during your marriage? That would be a car, a boat, savings, stocks or bonds, or anything?"

"The only thing that we have is a car. There is about $2,000 equity in that, and that's it. There is nothing else."

"Are any of the children yours or are they hers from her previous marriage?"

"All hers."

"Well, George, your situation is very simple. Anybody could handle it. This is my best shot. Get an inexpensive lawyer and give your wife the car."

"Isn't that like handing her a thousand dollars?"

"Not really. You see, if you decide to fight for the car or your share of it, you will spend that much anyway. Let's say that your lawyer costs $125 an hour. If you go to court and your case goes past the lunch hour, your lawyer will most likely charge you for the whole day. That's $1,000. Even if you win, you won't win anything. If you lose, which in your circumstances is very likely, you will lose $2,000. No matter how you look at it, you have nothing to gain by fighting for the car. Do you see what I mean, George?"

"I think so, pastor. So who should I go to?" he said in a subdued manner.

There was a newly graduated lawyer in our single-parent fellowship group who was well known (we thought) and had served in leadership of the group. I called him for George and broke ground for an appointment. Benedict, the lawyer, agreed with me that this one was cut and dried and should be a piece of cake.

George's last question to me was, "How much do you think this will cost me, pastor?"

"If you don't fight for anything and she doesn't, you should get out of this for under $300, I should think."

He nodded and left thoughtfully absorbed in our conversation. I didn't hear from George for three or four months. When I did, I was shocked to find that he was embroiled in a horrendous legal battle that was quite out of hand. It seems my friend, Benedict, the lawyer, was able to stir George's emotions to the boiling point and goaded him into fighting for the $1,000 equity in the car. One thing led to another, and a war broke out, replete with restraining orders, court dates, and dozens of lawyer and client conferences. As I had predicted, he lost the car and managed to spend some $7,000 doing it.

Benedict had charged him $140 an hour, so the bill ballooned quickly. I bet most of you have never seen a lawyer's billing sheet before. I have included the one from this case. This could be a preview of a coming attraction, so take the time to read through it and think about whether or not you want to obtain a lawyer. Notice that this one billing accounts for only $2,244 of the total bill, which ultimately grew to more than $7,000. The case went on for months and created a great deal of emotional turmoil for both parties above and beyond the extreme and unreasonable expense. Who's to blame? Two angry people, for sure, who let things get out of hand, and one clever, greedy lawyer who exploited the cultural differences between himself and his client and his client's wife. Note also that the bill only covers a two-and-a-half-week period from April 14 to May 2.

Lawyers are not the only dangerous players in this high-stakes game of life. The judges are pretty potent also. Although, for the most part, my experience observing judges has been a good deal more positive than with lawyers, I am still well within the mark to say there is no telling what judges will decide; even

ENCLOSED YOU WILL FIND: A corrected and amended itemized statement of account for April 14 to May 2.

ITEMIZED STATEMENT OF ACCOUNT
4–14 to 5–2

DATE	SERVICE	TIME	AMOUNT
4-3	Review of pleadings, declarations and points and authorities on motions	1.3*	$182.00
4-3	Phone consultation regarding wife's property from car	.1	N/C
4-3	Conference Re: Points and authorities	1.4	N/C
4-3	Preparation for client consultation	.3	$42.00
4-3	Client consultation regarding motion for reconsideration	1.3	$182.00
4-3	Complete points and authorities	1.5	$230.00
4-4	Proof points and authorities, conference	1.3	$182.00
4-4	Review of first draft on motion to vacate judgment	.5*	$70.00
4-4	File motion at Orange County Superior Court	.9	$126.00
4-7	Prepare SDT	1.3	$182.00
4-8	Phone consultation: Client Re: Notice from GMAC subpoenas	.2	$28.00
4-8	Prepare interrogatories	1.0	$140.00
4-8	Phone conference re: SDT	.1	N/C
4-9	Draft letter Review substitution of attorney	.5	$70.00
4-9	Prepare notice to produce	.6	$84.00
4-9	Phone conference: Attorney	.2	$28.00
4-9	Phone conference: Attorney	.3	$42.00

DATE	SERVICE	TIME	AMOUNT
4-10	Consultation	.1	N/C
4-10	Phone conference: Attorney Regarding ex parte notice	.1	N/C
4-11	Phone conference: Attorney	.2	$28.00
4-11	Phone consultation: Client	.1	N/C
4-11	Phone consultation: Client	.1	N/C
4-11	Phone consultation: Client	.2	$28.00
4-11	Draft letter	.5	$70.00
4-15	Phone conference: Attorney	.2	$28.00
4-12	Proof letter to Attorney	.1	N/C
4-21	Review response to motion to re-consider	.2	$28.00
4-22	Phone conference: Client	.2	N/C
4-25	Prepare for hearing	.8	$112.00
4-25	Hearing at Orange County Superior Court and Juvenile Court	2.5	$252.00
4-27	Phone consultation: Client	.1	N/C
4-17	Draft letter to attorney	.7	$98.00
4-18	Phone conference: Attorney	.3	$42.00
4-18	Dictate Local Rule 504 Declaration	.4	$56.00
4-18	Dictate letter to attorney	.6	$84.00

TOTAL CHARGES		17.8	$2,414.00
PREVIOUS BALANCE:			90.00
SUBTOTAL			$2,504.00
(CREDIT)			($1,410.00)
SUBTOTAL			$1,094.00
REQUIRED RETAINER			$720.00
TOTAL NOW DUE			$1,814.00

---

*Associate Attorney

PLEASE NOTE: Pursuant to the terms of your retainer agreement, please pay the above total amount due by 5-15. Thank You!

when you see that something is cut and dried, black and white, so much so that a child could make an intelligent ruling.

My friend Bill had fought and won primary custody of his children. This was not a normal event; normally only 3 percent of the men in the United States are awarded more than 50 percent of the time with their children. Bill had won because he had proven that his wife was taking their children into a very unstable environment. Her lover was an alcoholic given to violent fits of temper and had spent time in a mental institution. In the first trial the judge had taken the time to read carefully the Social Service Department's recommendation, which spelled out in detail the advantage the children would have being placed with their father. The second judge, an appeal judge, didn't read the report. He overturned the first decision, giving as his reason, "The children need a mother." Never had I witnessed blind justice quite so blind.

The sad truth is that if you decide to divorce your mate, you will need a lawyer and you will need a judge. Most people cannot make the important decisions necessary without their help. You will be paying lawyers by the hour, so it is in their best interests to prolong the proceedings. They have no real incentive to do their job quickly or expeditiously. The judges, on the other hand, are hard pressed for time, and your case is not likely to be given the time needed to make a fair and prudent or wise decision. The judges may also be bitter, sick and tired of hearing two people cut each other to pieces with words. They may not even be hearing anyone. They may be far more intuitive than cognitive.

Nothing is cut and dried and the most your lawyer can say is that you have a chance at obtaining what it is you perceive you need or have requested. The decisions are often arbitrary and capricious, subject to the eloquence of lawyers and the biases of judges. "Right" and "wrong" in our legal system are very subjective terms. *Don't count on justice in the divorce court.* It may happen, but don't count on it.

4

Will It Never End?

THERE IS A MYTHICAL FEELING that precedes a divorce: "When the divorce is over I can go on free from the influence of the person who brought so much pain into my life." That seems a reasonable feeling, but it never works out that way. You will be appalled and dismayed at the way your former mate keeps coming at you.

If you have children (and 70 percent of you do), you will be forced to talk to each other. You will arrange child visitation, vacation plans, holiday schedules, and inform each other when the children are sick or have some special problem. If something happens during your period of care, you will most likely be dealing with accusations concerning your irresponsibility and ineptness. By definition, a former mate is

someone who rarely if ever can do anything right.
After all—that's one of the reasons you separated.
Because of the anger levels achieved when someone
makes it clear that she or he no longer wants to have
anything to do with you, you may expect vengeful
behavior.

Vengeful behavior will come in many forms; the
most likely is further legal action. If your ex discovers
that your financial situation has changed for the better, you can be sure she or he will seek an adjustment
in child or spousal support. Your mate may force you
to fight for your support because she or he enjoys
provoking or punishing you.

Mark Twain said, "It takes two people to hurt you,
someone to say something bad about you and your
best friend to tell you what they said." You will be
hearing from several sources what a jerk you were.
You will be painted as a couch potato, immature, abusive, insensitive, neglectful, boring, unmotivated, and
useless. What will make this a more difficult cross to
bear is that you will be hearing these things from
well-meaning friends who you were hoping not to involve in your personal affairs. You will also hear from
people you don't care for, and about whom you feel
that this is none of their business anyway. Worst of all,
you will hear it from your children.

Children are the favorite weapon of choice and the
surest way to get to your former spouse. Even though
children should never be used in this way, it seems
impossible for parents to resist the temptation.

An eight-year-old girl asked her father if he really
loved her. He said, "Of course I do. Why do you ask?"

She said her mother had told her he hadn't wanted any more children after her older brother, and he never wanted her to be born. The father had thought that three children were sufficient for the family, but from the first time he had held his daughter in his arms, he was forever wrapped around her finger.

I'm sure you can imagine how he felt about what his ex-wife was telling their daughter behind his back. He had received primary custody, and this was said on the first visitation with the mother. He doesn't know what his daughter will be told or how she will be hurt, so he plans to debrief her after every visit with her mother. Try to imagine what life will be like for their daughter under this system. It is not ideal, to say the least.

Somehow the subject of your ex will keep coming up. When it does, you will find it conjures up old, dark feelings you thought would go away. My father was married and divorced long before I was born. His first marriage occurred when he was very young and in the Navy. The marriage didn't last very long, but it lasted long enough for him to have a tattoo of his first wife and her name indelibly imprinted on his left arm. The tattoo was a beautiful woman's profile. It looked like a 1920s cameo, and just underneath it was a banner. On the banner was inscribed "Boots."

I must have asked my father fifty times to tell me about the tattoo and something about the woman whom it portrayed, but he would not. He would always answer me the same way, "Son, this is just a reminder of something stupid I did when I was very young. That's all you need to know and that's all I'm going to say." My father died when I was fifteen, and Boots will forever remain a mystery because he never said anything more about her. I remember thinking even when I was young that his thinking about Boots made him very sad. This was more than twenty years since he had last seen her. I meet very few people who are ever completely free from the painful memories of going through a divorce.

If you divorce, there is a 95 percent chance you will remarry within five years, and as we have mentioned there is more than a 70 percent chance you will fail in your second marriage. The risk is even greater if you marry a third time. What I haven't said is why these remarriages fail. The leading cause of failure in a remarriage is the effect of the children. Children always remain loyal to their birth parents. They will inevitably cause trouble for stepparents.

Sheila is an attractive and vivacious woman who chose to marry a young handsome policeman. This was her first marriage and his second. He had two children by his first wife and was awarded visitation rights on every other weekend. His former wife has not yet remarried but was living with someone. His children, a boy and a girl, are normal and beautiful and both bear the scars that children of divorce bear. They are never really happy whether they are with their mother or with their father. They know consciously that their mother and father will never get back together, but they don't know it subconsciously. They have made life difficult for both of their parents, but especially for their father because he was the first to remarry. That, of course, makes it more difficult for the children to get their birth parents back together. But they try, especially the daughter.

During the first year of this new marriage, the children tested it in every possible way. There were moodiness, fighting, attempts to divide their father from their stepmother, and unkind notes designed to hurt her feelings. Things they said about their stepmother to their real mother led to problems, and it became increasingly difficult to look forward to the children's visits. Sheila viewed her stepdaughter as a vicious and calculating little shrew and was convinced she was actually bent on destroying the marriage. Now you need to know that when all this was happening, the little girl we are talking about was only eight years old.

The stepmother reached deep for new resolve. She became determined to form a friendship with the daughter. On a weekend that the father was called to Washington, D.C., Sheila picked up the children and planned a wonderful itinerary designed to demonstrate her desire to care for them and get to know them better.

The daughter noticed Sheila wearing her engagement and wedding rings on a gold chain around her neck. Sheila is a cosmetologist and was suffering an allergic, chemical reaction between her fingers. They were swollen and irritated and had not healed. The daughter asked Sheila why she was not wearing the rings, and Sheila gave her a thoughtful and complete explanation about how hairdressers work with irritating chemicals and that this sort of thing happens now and then. She also shared that she was anxious to be wearing the rings again as soon as possible. The daughter nodded and seemed to accept the explanation. This was on a Friday night.

On Sunday, Sheila invited the children to go with her to the airport to pick up their father. She would rather have gone alone, but she was trying to do her best to make the situation better between the three of them. The children sat on the benches staring at the door that their father would be coming through any minute. Finally, he came. The children both bounded forward, and the daughter arrived first. She could have said anything like, "I've missed you. Welcome home. How was your trip?" but she didn't. She blurted out, "Guess what? Sheila hasn't been wearing your wedding ring all weekend." The father looked dismayed, and Sheila's heart sank as she wondered what he must have been thinking at that moment.

That story is just an example of what the children of remarriage will do to you. There are many ways they will hurt you and color the atmosphere of your home. Expect to hear more than once, "You're not my real mother (or real father), so I don't have to mind you." You will tell them "no," and they will go straight to their real parent and ask the same question. A lot of the time they will get their way because a father who only sees his children once every two weeks finds it hard to say no.

You must remember that in a remarriage, parents are more closely bonded to their children than they are to their new mates, so they are apt to side with them, which will cause all manner of grief to new mates. They are all too often made to feel like outsiders. I have talked to dozens of new mates that tell me whenever the children come to visit, their mates completely check out on them and give all of their affection to the children, making them feel as if they are not even there.

To say that the effects of the divorce never end becomes an understatement in a remarriage. When a remarriage occurs, it is likely to be between a man who sees his children every other weekend and a woman who has custody of her children. It would not be unusual for this couple to have one of their own, so you end up with a yours-mine-and-ours situation. It is my observation that people never feel about another's children the way they feel about their own. More importantly, they don't treat them quite the same. This leads to all sorts of problems for the remarriages.

When blended families arrange for holidays, there can be scheduling nightmares. Holidays are times when you get together with your extended families. Let's say both you and your former mate get remarried. Your new mate has children, your ex-mate's mate has children, and all the grandparents are living. There could be four locations for children to go during the holidays. The children are not going to feel the same way about Christmas and Thanksgiving as they have in the past. Divorce wrecks holidays. They are never the same.

There is another myth we seem to carry with us as we go through life: that we learn from our mistakes. We really don't learn from our mistakes, we reinforce them. I think that is why we say, "There's no fool like an old fool." Sullen young men become grouchy old men. If you were not thoughtful or affectionate in your first marriage after the courtship, what makes you think you will be any more affectionate in your second? We want to believe we can change, but the truth is we rarely do. So we bring our weaknesses with us like unwanted baggage because they are part of who we are.

Another scary element to consider is that we tend to fall in love with the same kind of person we just divorced. If you despised a trait the first time around, how do you think you will react to it the second time around? I can tell you—violently. There will be a tendency to compare your first and second situations. If you see the similarities, you will become very uncomfortable, even panicked at times. This is called "transference." Because of transference, you may overreact to behavior that reminds you of your ex.

5

World War III

I DON'T KNOW IF THERE will ever be a third world war, but if there is, it will be like a divorce: explosive and damaging, and there are no winners. Remember, divorce is not an event, it is a process, and one that often seems endless. In that way it is more like the war in Vietnam. Vietnam went on and on and on and on and on . . . The issues were obscure, our soldiers did not receive the affirmation that they deserved, and the public was not supportive of the war because we were not sure that we should have been involved in it. Maybe divorce is more like the Vietnam War. Divorces go on and on and on and on . . . There are rarely heroes or villains. No one ever wins, and if they did, it would be after considerable wounding.

The list of the indignities suffered in a divorce are

staggering. When a divorce is declared it means the rejection of the one person in the world who best knows you. The thought that you will carry with you from that time on is, "When someone really gets to know the real me, I'll be rejected again." That is a scary thought.

Most of your friends will assume that it takes two people to cause a divorce. Whether you were innocent of wrongdoing or not, you will be judged. Married couples you were close with before the divorce will likely avoid you rather than take sides. Divorces are viewed as failures, and you will most likely feel like one and be made to feel like one. Every work application and form made seems to ask if you are married or divorced? These forms will mock you, and you will rarely be given a chance to explain your circumstances or vindicate yourself.

During the divorce process you will be made to disclose every wart in your life. There is hardly a personal question that will be left unasked. Your lawyer will ask you to reveal all your financial dealings for the last few years. If you have ever done anything shady, your mate is likely to make sure it comes to light. If a custody battle is enjoined, you and your mate will be probed by psychologists, and a lengthy report will be filed that can and will be used against you during the battle. People whom you considered to be friends will write letters that characterize you in a very bad light. I am talking about people whom you considered for years to be your friends.

The following is a letter written about a close friend of mine. I have known him for twenty years. I was best man in his wedding. My wife, Carol, and I have been in his home several times during his thirteen-year marriage. We have observed first hand the marital relationship, their relationship with their children, and were very aware of his relationship with his in-laws. The letter was written by his in-laws to help their daughter obtain custody of their two children. Read the letter, then let me tell you the situation.

The Letter

April 25

We submit the following in support of our belief that John is not fully capable of properly rearing his and Julie's two boys, Tom and Jim. We have been in close contact with him since his marriage to Julie, and over the past two years have noticed an increasing tendency toward depression and withdrawal, as evidenced by the following observations.

A. He frequently seems to be unaware of what is going on around him.

1. We have been passengers on more than one occasion in a car that he was driving and have been alarmed by his recklessness, which seemed to stem from his having his mind on other things.
2. We know that he has received several traffic tickets for unsafe driving in the past couple of years.
3. While driving a jeep on a back road in Panama last June with Julie, the boys, and us as passengers, he drove much too fast, plunging through puddles whose depths he could not judge, swerving around obstacles, jolting through ditches, and flinging us about at imminent risk of injury.

He seemed totally unaware that this was not normal behavior.

B. He continually ignores situations that are potentially dangerous to the boys or damaging to the property of others.

1. Many times, in fact, usually at our home, when the boys have been wild and rough, or when they have been engaged in activities that could be destructive to our property, John has made no move to deter them. Indeed, he seldom seems to notice what they are doing.

2. In Panama, in the home of friends whose house guests we were, John made no move to stop the boys when they were engaged in rough play that might have resulted in the breaking of valuable artifacts owned by the hosts.

C. He has difficulty communicating with us about ordinary things. Sometimes he is excited and voluble. Sometimes he sits with his head in his hands and is unresponsive. It is often hard to follow his train of thought. He skips from one thing to another. It is as if he leaves things out without realizing he has done so.

D. He appears unwilling and incapable of appreciating Julie's position in the problems that have arisen in their marriage.

1. Last summer, at the beach at Carpenteria, while celebrating Tom's birthday with several adult friends and a number of children and the two of us, he drew Julie away without a word to anyone and walked her far up the beach. They were gone forty-five minutes. We could see them, walking up and down the beach, his arm around her, his head bent—talking, talking, talking—stopping a

minute or two, and then walking on—talking. When they finally returned, Julie was in tears. It was the same as always, she said. He was displeased with her attitude. She didn't understand why.

2. During a three-week visit with friends in Panama last June, he isolated himself with Julie five or six times to continue the harangue. Each lasted thirty minutes or more.

E. On a morning hike, again in Panama, for no earthly reason that we could grasp, he became quiet and withdrawn. He walked away from the group and sat hunched on his heels with his head in his hands for fifteen or twenty minutes, while Julie and the boys waited nearby. The two of us walked back to the car to wait.

Myrtle and Buford

The Real Story

The statement concerning depression has some basis in truth. John was seeing his marriage dissolve even though they were in the midst of an expensive counseling process. He valued marriage and would have stayed in a bad one rather than divorce Julie. He would have done it for the children and, even more so, to be obedient to his faith. He was not given the chance.

John was accused of being unaware of what was going on around him. John is regarded as one of the most astute animal behaviorists in the world. Keen awareness is the quality that is most necessary to be good at determining animal behavior. John is one of the most observant people I've ever known, and

those that know him well would say that he never
misses a thing.

John was accused of having received several traffic
tickets in the last few years. John hadn't received any
during those years or since.

John was accused of reckless driving. I have driven
with John for twenty years and would describe him
as a slow driver on the verge of being too slow.

The accusation concerning whether John was a
good disciplinarian was interesting to me. On every
occasion that was mentioned, their daughter was
present, but the parents didn't accuse her or hold her
responsible for her sons' behavior in public. My opinion is that their boys were normal "all-boy boys," and
John was by far the superior controlling factor.

His in-laws omitted a lot of information. On the trip
to Panama mentioned in the court letter, John, at considerable risk to his own life, saved his in-laws' valu-
ables which had been stolen by a street gang, and he
was injured in the process. He also took care of all
their expenses on the trip. He was an ideal son-in-law,
and they knew it. The point is, people go crazy during
a divorce process and will say anything, true or false,
to help a relative or friend.

During the same divorce trial, another letter was
offered that cast John in a very awkward light. The
letter contained these statements.

Since Julie and her husband separated, I have
seen more of her and the boys. I have been to her
townhouse numerous times and have always found it

in order and clean. I have seen her interact with the boys on a daily, routine basis, and when it comes to day-to-day procedures, all children put up an argument and try to see what they can get away with. In my opinion, when they are with John, it's for a fun-filled weekend. Of course, John does not receive resistance from the boys when they are doing what they want and enjoy.

On one occasion when my son was playing with Jim, Jim described to him a movie he saw at his dad's house. The term he told my son was that he saw "naked people humping." Where was this caring, dedicated father while Jim was watching such a movie?

This could never have happened at John's house. His television was broken at the time. There were several other letters submitted that demeaned John's character and made him look foolish, disconnected, thoughtless, sexually permissive, mentally abusive, reckless, and irresponsible. John is my closest friend in the world and the finest Christian gentleman I know. He experienced these and dozens of other indignities during the two and a half years that they spent in the court process. All of these accusations were more true of his wife than true of him. He was vindicated at the end of this process by being given 57 percent of the child custody, but the war goes on and on and on and is not likely, in my mind, to end for years to come.

The following diary is designed to demonstrate the devastating process that you are likely to be

subjected to if you choose to divorce. Put yourself
in John's place as you read what it was like to experience a divorce.

August 26

Judy asked me for a legal separation today. So this
is the beginning of the end for our thirteen-year marriage. This didn't really come as a total surprise. It
was the logical conclusion to the past few years of
conflict and silence. It was all so gradual. I was fairly
sure this would happen to me and I am a bit surprised
that I am feeling so hurt. I'm not really sure why I
hurt so much. I'm not really sure that I love her any
more.

But I do know what this will do to our boys. It will
tear them to pieces. Maybe I'm angry because this
represents failure. So many hours in counselors' of-
fices. So much invested, for what? I guess I would do
it again. You have to try. I know that that's what God
would want. He knows how hard I tried. Maybe what
hurts is that my hopes of a happy family are gone. It
will never be the same.

I've seen other people who are divorced. Theirs is
not a bowl of cherries. I'm hurt and a little . . . no
that's not true, I'm plenty angry. The therapists were
able to provide a way for Judy to strip me of every
vestige of dignity that I had ever held onto. I don't feel
much like a man anymore.

I will wonder for a long time if Judy would have
continued to work on the marriage if the counselor
hadn't asked her if she had ever considered a trial
separation. She said that's what she would like and

left for eleven days. I told the therapist that I wanted to work on the marriage and didn't see a way to do that if we were separated. I still don't understand why a separation is supposed to help. It didn't help us. My boys are eight and ten. This will be horrible for them. I am powerless to stop it. This will just happen to us and I don't know what that is going to mean yet. I just know that my life is going to be full of complications and sorrow.

August 29

When Judy announced that she wanted to separate, she told me she was going to move out. She told me today she wants a divorce and she is not going to move out. My heart was filled with anguish when I realized I would be living in the same house with someone who doesn't want me any more. I will have a constant reminder that I am being set aside. She moved to one side of the house, leaving me to live on the other. There is almost no communication. Whatever communication exists is hostile. I think someone advised her not to move out. She wants the house; she wants everything. I think she thought she would lose the house for sure if she left, so she didn't.

I can see the confusion on my sons' faces. I am sure they don't understand. I don't understand. Their lives are in turmoil. Their mother tells them one thing about their future, and I am telling them another. None of us really have any idea of how it will be for sure. What future? It doesn't seem to me that we have a future. It will probably work out somehow.

We aren't the first ones that this has happened to,

but it's our first time, so it seems like our future is in question. How do you provide stability for your children when anger and resentment live just down the hallway? I don't know. She demanded that I leave the house. She said that she could force me if I wouldn't go on my own. I refused.

Dinner was sad tonight. For the first time it was fixed for three. There was nothing for me. Since the birth of our sons, it has always been dinner for four. I have felt lonely before, but now it was grabbing me and shaking me until I felt limp. I am being given a steady diet of rejection, and I am slipping into confusion and despair. [This was to last for ten weeks.]

I can now think of a thousand things that I would rather do than retain a lawyer. It meant coughing up hundreds of dollars that just weren't there and then laying my whole life out in front of him. I felt like a filleted fish, gilled and gutted. This was just the first meeting. I have been warned that the worst was yet to come. By the end of the meeting it seemed that my whole life was now written on a piece of legal-size lined paper for all to see. I felt naked; a feeling I have always hated. It was humiliating. [I later found out that this was the easiest hour of the process. The unknown would turn out to be a nightmare.]

October 28

Our first day in court. The battle is joined. I thought finances and property would be the first issues we would tackle, but I was wrong. It was custody. [I did not know for more than a year how this would be resolved.] I assumed Judy would agree to our sharing the custody of the children, fifty-fifty—but I was wrong. She had already agreed to the concept in conciliation court, but after talking to her lawyer she changed her mind. She demanded primary custody and insisted that I should be happy seeing them on a very restricted basis. I am sure this is strictly a financial move. I don't care about the finances. I just can't live with the idea of losing my boys.

It began to seem like everything that had ever meant anything to me was slipping away. I felt like I was sinking into a coma, a deep black coma. Consulting with my attorney was no comfort since he honestly explained there were no guarantees as to how judges would rule on custody matters. In fact, in a state where joint custody is supposed to be effected as often as possible, it is only awarded 11 percent of the time. Those weren't very good odds, but I am silently vowing to spend everything I am worth to be able to keep my boys. I will not let her do this to me. At least she won't do it easily. I was told only 3 percent of the men are awarded custody more than 50 percent of the time.

Who decides these things? Who has the right to say that boys need a mother more than a father? The reality was settling in, and it was crushing me. I turned to God. There was no place else to turn. He would help me. He surely knew my heart. He surely knew that they need me and I need them. Judy has forsaken her faith. How could He support her? He would be with me.

The court ordered a fifty-fifty arrangement for six months. They would spend one week with one parent, then one week with the other. It proved to be very disturbing for the boys. They just didn't understand why we were getting this divorce. How could they? Adults are supposed to have it together, be able to work it out. But we couldn't. Things were not going to get better. They made it clear that they wanted us back together. It tore me up to see them in such anguish. My youngest son asked me to buy a present for his mother; I didn't know what to say. I knew he was trying to get something started that would lead us to a reconciliation.

Several days later in that same courtroom, a ruling took place. For me it was a good-news, bad-news ruling. Judy was asked to leave the residence. That, of course, was the good news. I was also ordered to pay her $5,000 in ten days plus alimony and child support. I had no idea how I was going to pay $750 a month to Judy. At the end of the month I only had $300 to spare, and that had a way of being used for some emergency or unplanned need. I would worry about that later. For now I would try to be glad that I would only have to endure thirty more days of our joint loneliness. For this I am thankful. Thank you, Lord, for letting me see some relief.

November 5

At the urging of my closest friend I have begun attending the Single Parent Program at the First Evangelical Free Church in Fullerton. It is large but very warm and filled with people who have experienced divorce also. Some are like me, right in the middle of it, and some are through it and helping us to make it through. I feel less lonely when I go, which is almost every week now. Tonight was an especially good night at SPF. The drive to get home is about seventy-five miles, but it continues to be worth the drive because of the help and love I receive.

When I got home tonight at 1:30 A.M., I was to find my emotions devastated again. Every functional piece of furniture in our home had been removed. Debris was left for me to clean up. Nothing usable was left. A cloud descended as I walked through the house. I was filled with anguish the likes of which I had never known. This event had gone beyond the rejection stage to punishment.

The court had clearly stated that all the possessions would remain at the family residence until they were divided. My house was gutted. Only my bed and dresser remained, but Judy had removed the comforter, leaving just a sheet to protect me from the coldest day in November that I have ever or will ever know. To be fair, she left a broken dining room table and a broken chair. In the living room there was just a bean bag chair lying in the middle of the mess.

I didn't sleep tonight. I just laid there wondering why. I know there's no answer, but I cannot stop wondering. My head aches, my stomach feels hollow, and I'm tired to the bone. When will I stop feeling like I'm dying?

The boys' rooms were gutted. I don't know where they will sleep when they come tomorrow night. They have no bed, no toys, no books, no clothes. They don't have any reason to want to stay here. I may not be enough. They will probably want to go back to their mother's place after they see what it's like here. I would if I were a kid. I wish I was.

November 6

My heart pounded within me when I picked the boys up from school this afternoon. I wondered how they would react. When we got home we laid down on the floor because there was no place to sit. My oldest boy surveyed the empty room and asked, "Why did she do this, Dad?" How would you have answered that kind of question? The answer was too complex. I didn't really know. I think this was the lowest point for me in the whole process of the divorce. My boys had watched their mother, her parents, and two couples gut the house. They didn't like what was happening but, of course, were powerless to stop it. All three of us slept that night in my queen-sized bed. We comforted each other. It was a long time before I was to recover from the hurt of it.

December 8

Back to court. We hoped to get a lot accomplished today, but Judy didn't show up. I believe she was advised not to. We were going to ask the court to make her bring the furniture back, but everything was postponed. The day cost me $800, and nothing was accomplished at all. This was the first of twenty-two delays.

January 16

Back to court. We spent our time arguing in the halls. The justice building rumbled with our fighting. It was mostly over the furniture, which I ended up giving to her in hopes that she would be more reasonable about other issues. Maybe it would speed up the process, and the divorce would be over sooner. The only piece of furniture I insisted that I get back was a sofa. That was not easy. She actually told other people that she had been more than generous with the division of the household goods. My conciliation didn't help a thing. We were in court for two more years after this hallway discussion.

April 15

Back to court. This was to be the custody hearing. I was still hoping my wife would agree to joint custody, but she would not have it. She wanted the boys to be divided. She would take one and I would take one. I wouldn't hear of it. Judy pushed for a court-ordered psychological examination and evaluation of both parents. This would add six more months to the process and cost $3,000. The divorce was taking its toll on me emotionally, physically, and financially. To date nothing had been resolved about anything and all the main issues were still up in the air. Will it ever end? I am on empty—past empty. No, I can't be; I'm still going.

The child and spousal support was raised to $1,200 a month, which meant I would have to find ways of borrowing $900 a month from someone because $1,200 was $900 more than I made. Because we are still in a custody battle, I have to pay every cent of child support demanded. If I don't, it would look like the only reason I wanted the children was to keep from paying child support. The court ordered me to pay all the debts, court costs, and legal fees.

July and August

The psychological testing began. My sons hate being taken out of school. They hate the psychological testing. They know deep down that they are choosing whom they want to be with. No child should be forced to make that choice. But they would be. I hope that they choose me. Each of us went in alone, then each parent with each son, then each parent with both sons, then both parents with both sons, then both parents without the sons. All of our lives were exposed for someone to meddle with, but there was no other way, and I would not turn back. The choice was now in someone else's hands. Someone would be telling me how much time I would be spending with my sons. I hope they are kind. I hope they are good.

In addition to the tests, we submitted letters from friends and other qualified persons who knew us and our situation. I later found out that letters Judy's friends submitted said I exposed my children to pornographic material. I hate pornographic material and would die rather than have my sons exposed to it. I was also accused of being a poor driver, even though I have not received a ticket in years and years. Her friends testified that I was a very poor parent. Even though I know none of these things is true, I wonder if someone might believe them.

October 28

Thank you, Lord! I was awarded 57 percent of the custody. My prayers have been answered. The visitation arrangements have been a nightmare to work out. Dealing with Judy has continued to be a battle.

John and Judy continued to battle and are battling still. To date they have spent $30,000 on legal expenses alone. They still fight on the phone, and the boys are still bearing the effects of the divorce. The divorce is final, but a new court date has been scheduled to modify child support.

Divorce is just like World War III—only it never ends.

6

It's Not Good That Man Should Be Alone

THE NUMBER-ONE FEELING that prevails when a person decides to divorce is a deep and pervasive feeling of loneliness. It hangs over you like an arctic winter. Cold winds of despair, dampened hopes, and cloudy feelings each in their turn steal hope, leaving their hosts with the assurance that they will never experience the gentle caress of another spring. The loneliness cuts like a knife. It twists and turns, and the pain can be relentless and unbearable. This turns out to be true for both the person that leaves the marriage as well as the one who is left. Those who leave usually leave to pursue an affair. They are at first caught up in the exhilaration of sexual adventure. But every adventure becomes commonplace after awhile, and the participants in affairs rarely marry. If they do, they are usually divorced within a five-year period. They are often more miserable than the partners whom they first abandoned—they have to deal with two marriage failures, and the guilt compounds as they leave damaged lives in their wake.

The loneliness can become very intense. Thoughts of suicide become all too common, although they are rarely acted upon. I was introduced to the power of loneliness by one of my favorite single parents. Her story moved me beyond any story that I have heard to date.

Gail came to my office one day seeking pastoral counsel. I was brand new and very unprepared to hear what she had been through. The story that she shared was the story of a woman who had been to hell and back. By God's grace alone she had lived to tell the story.

She seemed very much at peace, very together as we began the introductory chitchat that unfolds as two people meet for the first time. She shared that she had come to Southern California from Wyoming. She very much appreciated being a part of our single parents fellowship. I expressed how glad I was that she was coming and asked how I might be able to help her. She shared that she needed someone to help her gain perspective on a decision that she was making. The amenities out of the way, she began to tell a story that I will never forget.

"I was a pastor's wife; he's not a pastor anymore, and we're now divorced. He's been calling and writing lately and he says that he wants to get back together."

"And you're wondering if that would be possible or wise?" I asked as she paused momentarily.

"Yes, that's the question," she answered.

"What led to your getting a divorce?"

"Jack and I were married for twenty years when I discovered that he was having an affair. I was of course deeply hurt and began to confront him about it. I asked him how he could commit adultery and still call himself a Christian. This really struck a sharp chord because he became red faced. He slapped me and pushed me down on the floor. Then he screamed at me. This type of thing happened frequently, and Jack became progressively more violent. One night he threw me down on the floor and held his hand over my mouth so I couldn't breathe. He pushed down so hard that he broke one of my front teeth. These incidents were horrible, but not as horrible as having him tell me that he had broken off the affair and discovering that he hadn't. Jack is still in that relationship, and they are living together in San Diego. They've been together for four years now."

"He's living with the other woman and has been writing to you about getting back together?" I asked, seeking clarification.

Gail put her head down, then looked up and said, "Yes, that's right."

"Aren't you a little skeptical?" I asked.

"Well, yes."

"How can you even be considering taking him back?" I asked with genuine amazement.

"I'm very lonely," she offered in deep humility.

"Gail, let me recount to you what you have just

shared with me. Jack has sustained a long-term affair, repeatedly hit you, suffocated you, broke one of your teeth, and lied to you over and over, so there is no way that you could possibly trust him. Are you telling me that your loneliness is harder to endure than that?"

I was floored when she said, "Sometimes."

I couldn't think of anything to say. I have never been that lonely. When God said, "It is not good that man should be alone," He must have meant it in a deeper way than I could either understand or imagine. Gail tells me that I ministered to her that day; perhaps it was for no other reason than she could sense how much I was moved by her story and her profound loneliness. Since then I have seen and felt that same vacuum in hundreds of people. None have shared it quite as clearly as Gail, but I'm sure that they felt it just as deeply.

I have had the opportunity to meet Gail's former husband and to talk to him. He was still living with the other woman, but he had long since fallen out of love with her. Not having anywhere to go, he simply shared space with her rather than face life alone. He had no close friends. Gail was not ready to trust him. His children despised him. Although he was not able to share it, I knew by intuition that his loneliness was every bit as cancerous as Gail's. It was eating him alive.

Their children were affected deeply. Both of their sons have withdrawn from their faith in Christ, and their daughter was in counseling to be helped for her inability to trust men. Gail shared a private and touching moment that she had experienced with her youngest son. He confessed that he had been thinking seriously about committing suicide. She admitted to him that she had considered suicide. Then together they made a pact never to give in to their feelings because they loved each other too much.

The loneliness that follows divorce is excruciatingly painful and comes at a time when you most need to be loved and supported. It leaves its victims willing to alter their value system if they think a change of behavior will bring them relief. I cannot begin to number the dear people who have confessed to me that after their divorce they began drinking, even if they had never done so before. Many, both men and women, initiate sexually intimate relationships in an attempt to feel close to someone again. They only confirm that sex is not love and feel more alone and abandoned than ever. Many men have confessed to me that they were caught up in pornographic literature and videos following their divorce. They were trying to meet their perceived sexual needs. The pornography only heightened their feelings of loneliness and added to the feeling that they were adrift in a fog-shrouded ocean. There was water everywhere, but no matter how much they drank, it never quenched their thirst.

Many hit the bar scene, which at least offered some human companionship. They sat in semi-darkness, filled with hollow laughter and shallow conversation, hoping somehow to make a connection with someone, anyone who really cared if they lived or died. Maybe they went there to dull their pain. Their dreams were rarely realized. A bar is no place to mine gold, although it may pay off like a slot machine that keeps you believing that the jackpot is a quarter away. Many stay home to dull the pain. They also let their doctor write prescriptions for loneliness. But family and committed friends are the only cure. No pill, no one-night stand, or any other empty pursuit will do anything but expand the problem. One futile day will chase the next until life begins to pass without color or meaning.

Many single-parent mothers have shared that their self-imposed exiles were ended when they became starved for adult conversation and companionship. They didn't want to be divorced or hang out with divorced people, but their loneliness drove them out for need of friendship, an adult voice or a touch.

You need to know that divorce leads to loneliness as sure as Saturday leads to Sunday.

7

Is Divorce Ever the Appropriate Course?

ONE OF THE DIFFICULT ASPECTS of being a single-parent pastor is that I have been asked weekly the question, "Am I sinning if I file for a divorce?" I tremble when I answer that question because I know that as a pastor I am speaking on God's behalf. The Book of Deuteronomy makes it quite clear that when a prophet presumes to speak the words that the Lord has not said, he should be stoned. So I never ever answer that question lightly. I do answer, however, and the criteria that I try to keep in mind when I do are as follows:

1. Does God speak clearly to this issue in His word? If He does, then there is no problem. I merely share what God has said and encourage

the person to be obedient and trust that God would know best concerning their question.

2. If there is no clear answer to the question being asked, I search for related scripture and do my best to apply the wisdom that God has given me and pray that I am representing His will.

3. When answering, I try to view the person to whom I am speaking as if he or she were my son or my daughter. The reason I do this is that God has a father's heart. He is compassionate. Our human intellect is simply not sufficient to make the most important of judgments. We need to temper our intellect with our feelings. If Jesus had exercised only cold intellect on the woman caught in adultery, He would have picked up the first stone. She was caught, and she was guilty. He knew things we didn't and found room for compassion. Compassion will lead us to better decisions based on a broader perspective.

4. If I don't know what I would do, I say, "I don't know what I would do." The problem for the Christian community is that it can find the answer it wants to hear. There are pastors that support every point of view. There are pastors that will take the position that divorce is never appropriate. And there are pastors that say God's grace is sufficient to cover any action even intentional rebellion.

In the final analysis, what really matters is what God thinks. He has promised His Holy Spirit to convict of sin if we're sinning. A good rule concerning sin is, "When in doubt, don't." If there is a shred of doubt that you are violating God's will, then you will lose nothing by waiting to make the decision. You will certainly win God's approval, not to mention peace of mind. The heart of what I am saying is don't make this decision quickly. Give God the time to move in your situation or make His will clear to you.

Now let me commit myself, realizing that no matter what I say I will own critics. I believe there are three legitimate causes for divorce, and they are as listed below:

1. Adultery
2. Abuse (physical to spouse or children)
3. Abandonment

I see these as legitimate reasons for a person to seek a divorce, and I believe in my own heart that no sin would be involved and God would not be found in an irritated posture. None of my list would mandate a divorce or even recommend one either. I believe that persons whose mates have abandoned them, abused them, or committed adultery would be permitted to divorce if they desired to do so.

You may ask, "Is there a scripture that substantiates your position that physical abuse is a legitimate reason to divorce your mate." There is no direct scripture, but there is related scripture. Consider the following:

"Husbands, love your wives, as Christ loved the church and gave Himself up for her, that he might sanctify her, having cleansed her by the washing of water by the word, that he might present the church to himself in splendor, without spot or wrinkle or any such thing, that she might be holy and without blemish. Even so husbands should love their wives as their own bodies. He who loves his own wife loves himself. For no man ever hates his own flesh but nourishes and cherishes it, as Christ does the church, because we are members of his body. For this reason man shall leave his father and mother and be joined to his wife, and the two shall becomes one flesh. This mystery is a profound one and I am saying that it refers to Christ and the church; however, let each one of you love his wife as himself, and let the wife see that she respects her husband" (Eph. 5:25).

There is simply no room for physical abuse in this passage. The choice for divorce would be like Hobson's choice, "The lesser of two evils." Wouldn't it be grand if all our choices were black and white or right and wrong. It would so simplify life. But we are often faced with two evils, and our best bet is to minimize our losses.

I believe that Lewis Smedes spoke rightly when he said, "This is not to say that God approves of divorce; it is only to say that He sometimes disapproves of its alternatives even more than he disapproves of divorce."

You will not be excused from a sin if you obtained poor counsel—Eve wasn't. You must stand or fall on the merits of your own decisions. So make your choices with care.

I serve on the staff of a large and conservative evangelical church. We make no apology for trusting God's word. We rely on it to the degree that we understand its exact demands. I'm not sure that any of us on our staff feel that we can say with the Apostle Paul that we understand all spiritual mysteries, but we try. I thought it would be interesting to list a number of hypothetical questions dealing with divorce and let our staff comment on whether or not they felt that a divorce was a viable option. If they felt that scripture applied, they were asked to share it. If they felt that a comment was necessary, they could also share it. You shouldn't look at the results of this poll of pastors as possible counsel. The idea behind the poll is to demonstrate that different points of view are likely even in a homogeneous group of unified pastors. If any are unanimous, it may indicate that the scripture was clear on the topic.

1. Bill came to us distraught. He had just been informed by his wife that she had been in a long-term affair with his best friend. She told him she wanted a divorce but wanted him to file. She also informed him that his best friend had just served his wife with divorce papers. When the divorces were final, she intended to marry his best friend. Bill said he didn't want her back, but he was afraid to file for divorce because God might be angry with him if he did. Bill's question is, "Is divorce permissible?"

Yes	No	Not sure
86 percent	7 percent	7 percent

2. Vicky has been married for ten years. Nine of the ten years her husband has periodically abused her and their children. The abuse was severe: broken teeth, broken bones, and a concussion. Vicky says she

has no more love for her husband, but she is afraid that God will abandon her if she files for divorce. She asks, "May I divorce my husband?"

Yes	No	Not sure
64 percent	22 percent	14 percent

3. Bonnie had been married for seven years. She had three children. She came home one day to find a note on the television. It read, "Dear Bonnie, I can't handle it anymore. I have to go find happiness before it's too late." He signed it, "Forgive me, Bob." It has been eighteen months since Bonnie and the children have heard anything from Bob. Bonnie had gone on welfare and moved back in with her parents. Bonnie's question was, "Pastor, I've accepted the fact that Bob doesn't want us anymore. Is it all right if I file for a divorce?"

Yes	No	Not sure
43 percent	36 percent	21 percent

4. Judy had been married for fourteen years. Six months into the marriage, Bruce began drinking to relax, then he began drinking to get through the day. He had difficulty keeping jobs. During the last three years he was unemployed more than employed. He made Judy go to work and yelled at her if she didn't keep the house up as she had when she hadn't worked. He never did any housework or yardwork himself. Bruce alienated all of their friends. Her life became, as she put it, "Full of every shade of gray you could imagine." She had long since given up begging

Bruce to get help and had herself given up on Bruce. She wanted something more from life than she had gotten and asked, "Pastor, is it wrong to seek a divorce? I just can't take anymore." Can she divorce?

Yes	No	Not sure
8 percent	62 percent	30 percent

5. Jack had married Carmen just out of high school. The truth is that he had gotten her pregnant and felt that it had been the honorable thing to do. For years he had resented the fact that he had missed the care-free days of college and that true love was not the foundation for their relationship. He had finished college through night school and during the process distanced himself from Carmen. His work and school left little time for their relationship. Besides, there was quite an intellectual gulf between them. Eight years and three children later he shared with his pastor, "Pastor, I'm sure I missed God's best somewhere. Our marriage was never based on love and we've grown apart through the years. God couldn't want anyone to feel the way I feel. I think it would be in everyone's best interests if I just left. She could find someone that would love her the way she is and I could find someone that I could grow with. Don't you think it would turn out all for the best?"

Yes	No	Not sure
0 percent	100 percent	0 percent

6. June just discovered that her husband is having an affair with another man. He says he is not sure if

he is homosexual or bisexual and he can't guarantee that he won't act out his homosexuality from time to time. He assures June that he loves her and she is not the problem. June wants out of the marriage.

Yes	No	Not sure
93 percent	7 percent	0 percent

7. Jeff admits to Sharon that he had a one-night stand on a business trip. He begs her forgiveness and assures her that the woman meant nothing to him and he would never do anything like that again. He implores her not to leave him, but she has been unable to forgive him nor can she get it out of her mind. They have two children, three and five. She shares with her pastor, "I just can't get this thing out of my mind. Would God understand if I filed for divorce? Can I divorce Jeff?"

Yes	No	Not sure
14 percent	86 percent	0 percent

8. Frank is in a mess. After twenty-five years of marriage, his wife has become severely mentally ill. Her disease is paranoid schizophrenia. She has become very delusional and is progressively less able to deal at any rational level. The children are suffering greatly from her neglect and irrational behavior in front of their friends. She has alienated all of their close adult friends and they haven't slept in the same bedroom for five years. Frank has made repeated attempts to get help, but without success. You cannot

commit a person to a mental institution against her or his will unless they cannot find their way home or are a danger to themselves and to those around them. Frank cannot handle the strange behavior, the loneliness, and the damage to the children. He feels that if they are not to be permanently damaged by their mother's abnormal behavior, he must divorce his wife. What do you think? Does Frank have a basis for divorce?

Yes	No	Not sure
29 percent	43 percent	28 percent

9. Dirk and Kim have argued since the first week of their marriage. Their five years together have become a verbal reenactment of the Civil War, only much more relentless. Each has threatened the other repeatedly with divorce. Neither is happy, nor do they want to be married to each other. Professional counseling has been tried on three different occasions, but the sessions usually were used to carry on the battle. Kim wants out. She says, "Pastor, it's never going to change with us. We are oil and water; we'll never mix. We don't love each other anymore. My friend told me I would go to hell if I divorced Dirk, and I shared that hell might be an improvement. I don't know what happened, but I have to get out of this nightmare or I'm going to crack. Will God let me out of this? Please tell me He will."

Yes	No	Not sure
0 percent	100 percent	0 percent

10. Dave and Lisa have been married ten years. Every outward sign would indicate that everything is better than average, but Dave feels cheated. He is much more desirous of sexual activity than Lisa and has felt rejected when she says, "No, not tonight." He contends that she has taken away his manhood through ten years of reluctant behavior. He views this as a problem of submission.

Yes	No	Not sure
0 percent	100 percent	0 percent

As I guessed before the survey, there was not total agreement, even among a unified staff. So let me repeat, the divorce decision is yours and yours alone. The best you can hope for is to gather wisdom so when you make your decision you are making it on the strongest possible foundation.

John MacArthur once said, "When you want God's will with all your heart, what you want is most likely God's will. . . . Wise men still seek Him and those that seek Him long enough are promised to find Him. Take a lot of time with this decision. Time does not make anything right or wrong, but taking it ensures that more sides of the question can be examined. That alone would have to lead you to a better decision."

8

How Does God
Feel about Divorce?

ANYONE WHO BELIEVES IN GOD is at some point faced with the question, How does God feel about divorce? If your thoughts concerning God are based on little more than your own perceptions, then you will ultimately make Him feel as you do. He will always come to see it your way because you have made Him in your own image. You will invariably make Him in your own image so you can call the shots. He will always be subject to your thoughts about what He thinks. Your self-conceived God will always be obedient to what you think He thinks.

If you are a Christian, you believe that you have been made in His image and are subject to what He thinks as those thoughts are expressed in His written word, the Bible. You needn't bother about having an opinion in matters already made clear. When God has expressed His thoughts on a subject we needn't persist in having an opinion. Ours would be wrong anyway.

God has expressed His opinion clearly and concisely in the Bible. A summary statement on this subject could be, "God has a low view of aloneness, a high view of marriage, and He hates divorce."

First consider aloneness. Read the following passage:

> Then the Lord God said, "It is not good for the man to be alone; I will make a helper suitable for him." So the Lord caused a deep sleep to fall upon the man, and he slept; then He took one of the ribs, and closed up the flesh at that place. And the Lord God fashioned into a woman the rib which He had taken from the man, and brought her to the man. And the man said, "This is now bone of my bones and flesh of my flesh; She shall be called woman, because she was taken out of man." For this cause a man shall leave his father and his mother, and shall cleave to his wife; and they shall become one flesh (Gen. 2:18–24).

This passage brings us the very first assessment of our needs and personality. "It is not good for a man to be alone." Thus our statement that God has a low view of aloneness.

To answer loneliness, God created the institution of marriage. It is meant to fill man's needs; to complete him, and no relationship can do that any better than the way which the union of man and woman can.

There is nothing as satisfying as a good marriage nor as devastating as a bad one.

I have a friend whose marriage has deteriorated over the last seven years. For the last three years, he and his wife have maintained separate bedrooms. It appears at this point that the marriage is over and that nothing short of a miracle of God will save it from divorce. My friend says that occasionally he will awaken in the early morning hours and find his wife sitting at the foot of his bed. She doesn't make a sound as she slumps silently with her head in her hands. Her tears stain her night gown as she steals a little of the presence of the husband whose love she has killed, and she dies a little herself as the dawning reality of the impending break-up gnaws at her troubled soul and broken heart.

One night frightened by her presence he asked, "What are you doing?" She answered quietly, "I'm so lonely." He wanted to hold her, but he couldn't raise her hopes that everything was going to be all right. It wasn't going to be, and soon they would be speaking through lawyers and fighting for the custody of their five children.

In the same way that a bad marriage is a kind of hell, a good marriage is a kind of heaven. Harold and Gertrude are retired missionaries. They served the Lord in Korea, and those that knew him well, thought of him as a modern-day Paul. He certainly has played a key role in the Korean revival, and his service led to the saving of hundreds of thousands of souls to the kingdom of Christ. He was in his eighties when

I asked him, "Harold, what was the best part of your life?" He said with a definite twinkle in his eye, "Next to meeting Jesus, meeting Gertrude. She has made my life pretty special." They were holding hands when I asked that question, which wasn't unusual because they were always holding hands. Think of it, more than fifty years of happy marriage, a little bit of heaven on earth, wouldn't you say?

Anything that has an extraordinary potential for happiness has an equal potential for disaster. The high view of marriage comes from the scripture just quoted and one other. In Genesis we see that marriage is valued and held in higher estate than the relationship that we have with our parents. Thus God says, "Leave your father and mother and cleave to your wife."

The other passage that illustrates just how highly God esteems the institution of marriage is from Ephesians.

Be subject to one another out of reverence for Christ. Wives, be subject to your husbands, as to the Lord. For the husband is the head of the wife as Christ is the head of the church, his body, and is himself its Savior. As the church is subject to Christ, so let wives also be subject in everything to their husbands. Husbands, love your wives as Christ loved the church and gave himself up for her, that he might sanctify her, having cleansed her by the washing of water with the word, that he might present the church to himself in splendor, without spot or wrinkle or any such thing; that she might be holy and without blemish. Even so husbands should love their wives as their own bodies. He who loves his wife loves himself. For no man ever hates his own flesh, but nourishes and cherishes it, as Christ does the church, because we are members of his body. 'For this reason a man shall leave his father and mother and be joined to his wife, and the two shall become one flesh.' . . . Let each one of you love his wife as himself, and let the wife see that she respects her husband (Eph. 5:21–32).

There is no greater reason for saying that God holds marriage in high esteem than that found in verse 32. The verse clearly states that in a mysterious way our marriages represent the way Christ relates to the church. Paul refers to this truth as profound, which is another way of saying that it is very important. God holds marriage in such high esteem that the most pleasurable human experience, sexual intercourse, is reserved for those that are married. It is not approved by God in any other context.

It is also clear that God hates divorce. This is asserted in no uncertain terms in the Book of Malachi: "For I hate divorce says the Lord the God of Israel, and covering ones garments with violence, says the Lord of hosts. So take heed to yourselves and do not be faithless" (Mal. 2:16).

I think you will be interested in the context of this verse; namely, what was being said to God's people and why such a shockingly blatant attack on divorce. First, the statement was directed to priests who should have known better. God was expressing His anger on a variety of topics related to the quality of worship He was receiving from His people.

In the first chapter of Malachi the Lord pointed out that they were not taking Him seriously. They neither treated Him as a father or a master. They would respect a father and be in awe of a master. He pointed out to them that they were no longer giving their best at sacrifice time. They were offering animals that no one would want, that no one would buy. In some cases they were bringing sheep that they had stolen from others as a sacrifice fit for the Lord. A verse that sums up God's assessment of their faith is found in the latter part of the chapter: "What a weariness this is, you say and you sniff at me, says the Lord of hosts" (Mal. 1:13). God was saying that the people were treating Him as food which they sniffed to see if they were going to want to eat it or not. God would not allow anyone to consider His will an option. Listen to the beginning of the second chapter.

"And now, O priests, this command is for you. If you will not listen, if you will not lay it to heart to give glory to my name, says the Lord of hosts, then I will send a curse upon you and I will curse your blessings; indeed I have already cursed them, because you do not lay it to your heart" (Mal. 2:1).

The most frightening verse follows: "Behold I will rebuke your offspring, and spread dung in your faces, the dung of your offerings, *and I will put you out of my presence*" (Mal. 2:3, emphasis added).

This is just what God did. He was not on speaking terms with His people for four hundred years. What exactly were the specific actions that caused the break in the relationship between the Lord and His people? There were probably more issues than surface in this powerful little book, but the major points of division were:

1. A high rate of divorce.
2. They were teaching only the parts of God's Word that they felt like teaching.
3. They were into the occult.
4. Adultery was rampant.
5. The poor were going neglected and no one was concerned for the needs of widows and orphans.
6. The priests were telling the people that doing evil was no real problem.
7. The people were not giving the minimum 10 percent that they had been commanded to give.
8. The priests were teaching that there was not real benefit in serving the Lord. This led the people to believe that it may be to their advantage to do evil in order to prosper.

That is of course a formidable list of evil things that His people were doing. Yet as evil as each individual sin was, it was divorce that God held up as the sin that He hates. What about divorce is so terrible? Let me give you a little more background to the situation in order to make the answer to the question meaningful.

The Jews had been dispersed among the surrounding nations and had fallen into many of the customs of those nations. The surrounding nations held a low view of marriage, and the men viewed their wives as primarily existing to produce children and bring them pleasure. The foreign women were raised to accommodate their men's perceptions of marriage and were satisfied for the most part to play out their role.

The Jewish women were raised with a broader role and God had made it clear that marriage was intended to be a till-death-do-us-part arrangement. The rabbis eroded this teaching to the point that a man could obtain a divorce for almost any reason. In the prophecies of Malachi we see the disintegrated family. The priests, whose job it would have been to preserve the family, were bailing out on their own marriages to marry foreign women. The foreign women were trained to be finer sexual partners, and I think this became the primary reason for the priests' leaving the wives of their youth. Only men could divorce; women had no say so. The women were held up to shame and even forced to give up their children. When the priests remarried, they would leave the raising of their children to the foreign women they had married. The women would of course raise the children in their traditions and teach them to worship their gods and follow their teachings. Human sacrifice and temple prostitution were practiced in most of the surrounding nations and Israel could not seem to resist the temptation to follow their customs.

Divorce has found its way into a select number of the things God hates. Only twelve are mentioned, and I think it is wise to know what they are. I have no desire to get on God's bad side, and doing the things that He hates would go a long way to getting me there. Remember the last time Israel got on His bad side, God chose not to speak to them for four hundred years. His concluding words in the Old Testament were: "Behold I will send you Elijah before the great and terrible day of the Lord comes. And he will turn the hearts of the fathers back to the children and the hearts of the children to the fathers, lest I smite the land with a curse" (Mal. 4:5–6).

It's easy to discern what the verse means. Fathers must not be caring about their children if they were anxious to have them raised by foreign women. God had made it clear earlier in the book that He desired Godly offspring. The foreign wives, however, were raising His children to worship other gods. For the children, hating their fathers was a natural consequence of sending their real mothers away.

The first words spoken after the four-hundred-year silent treatment were spoken by the angel Gabriel to an aging priest as he stood in the temple making an offering for Israel's sins. His name was Zechariah, and he was married to an also-aged woman by the name of Elizabeth. That they were both very righteous and happily married, is my guess, but they were childless, which was tragic because they both had so much to give. The Gospel records this event: "Gabriel said, 'Do not be afraid Zechariah, for your prayer is heard, and your wife Elizabeth will bear you a son, and you shall call his name John. And you will have joy and gladness, and many will rejoice at his birth. For he will be great before the Lord, and he shall drink no wine nor strong drink, and he will be filled with the Holy Spirit, even from his mother's womb. And he will turn many of the sons of Israel to the Lord their God, and he will go before him in the spirit of Elijah, *and turn the hearts of the fathers to the children*'" (Luke 1:12–17, emphasis added).

Does the Lord sound like He's softened any on the divorce issue after four hundred years? I don't think so. That would be one of the first issues His new Elijah would address. Remember that John the Baptist was beheaded for speaking out against Herod's immoral marriage to his brother's wife. The Lord considered this issue so important that he allowed one of his favorite men to be sacrificed for it.

What about Jesus? Was He soft on divorce? Let's find out. There is no statement in the scripture that speaks with more clarity on the issue of divorce than one found in Matthew's Gospel:

> And some Pharisees came to Him, testing Him, and saying, "Is it lawful for a man to divorce his wife for any cause at all?" And He answered and said, "Have you not read, that He who created them from the beginning made them male and female, and said, 'For this cause a man shall leave his father and mother, and shall cleave to his wife; and the two shall become one flesh?' Consequently they are no longer two but one flesh. What therefore God has joined together, let no man separate." They said to Him, "Why then did Moses command to give her a certificate and divorce her?" He said to them, "Because of your hardness of heart, Moses permitted you to divorce your wives; but from the beginning it has not been this way. And I say to you, whoever divorces his wife, except for immorality, and marries another woman commits adultery." The disciples said to Him, "If the relationship of the man with his wife is like this, it is better not to marry" (Matt. 19:1–12).

Did you notice the disciples reaction to Jesus' teaching? They felt it was harsh and certainly foreign to what they understood about marriage. The divorce problem was not yet solved, and they were under the impression that you could divorce your wife for just about any reason. When Jesus told them that immorality was the only permissible reason, their reaction was "Lord, if this is the only reason then it would be better never to marry at all." I'm sure they were thinking, "What if she's a nag, or stupid? What if she is a poor homemaker or a lousy lover?" They couldn't imagine getting stuck in those kinds of relationships. But the Lord did not waver from his high view of marriage and his hatred of divorce.

The Apostle Paul doesn't equivocate on the issue either. Again we see a high view of marriage and a disdain for divorce. "But to the married I give instructions, not I, but the Lord, that the wife should not leave her husband (but if she does leave, let her remain unmarried, or else be reconciled to her husband), and that the husband should not send his wife away. But to the rest I say, not the Lord, that if any brother has a wife who is an unbeliever, and she consents to live with him, let him not send her away. And a woman who has an unbelieving husband, and he consents to live with her let her not send her husband away."

If you are looking for any other position other than God hates divorce, you will not find it in the scripture. Cover to cover, God has a low view of aloneness, a high view of marriage, and He hates divorce.

After considering God's hatred for divorce, I was moved to determine what other things God hated. I was surprised to note that the hate list was relatively short, it had a total of only twelve items. I was also surprised to discover that all twelve were present in almost every divorce situation I have ever counseled. Let me take you through the list.

1. *God hates "Haughty eyes"* (Prov. 6:17). The idea in the proverb is that God takes no pleasure in people who look down on other people. He especially hates conceit or the attitude that people might consider themselves better, more worthy, or more deserving, than someone else. This way of thinking is usually present in the attitude of the person calling for the divorce without a biblical cause.

A close friend of mine stole his wife's diary to find out why he was being divorced. His wife would not discuss it with him, and he really did not understand why this was happening. She recorded her every feeling in her diary and he was sure that by reading the diary he could determine the exact cause of this horrible turn of events. He was right. He read through the diary and her thoughts emerged. She said in any number of ways that she viewed him as an inadequate spouse. She viewed him as a shallow jock incapable of understanding the finer things in life—those being the opera, the classics, the theater, and fine poetry. After outlining his deficiencies, she actually wrote that she felt "it was time that she traded upwards in mates." It sounded like she was trading in a car, a Hyundai for a Mercedes.

I have never seen it articulated in such a bold manner before, but I have seen the attitude displayed hundreds of times. It is simply the attitude that my happiness is more important than your happiness or the children's happiness or anybody's happiness. We have falsely obtained the idea that we have a right to be happy. If our happiness is to be purchased at the price of disobedience to God, then we have gone too far. Disobedience never produces happiness anyway. It produces guilt by the Holy Spirit. Sin will never provide what it promises. It only provides the painful reality that we have missed the best. We have missed the mark.

2. *"God hates a lying tongue"* (Prov. 6:17). Every married person I know made promises in front of witnesses and before God. The promises were of the solemn and contractual variety and usually included phrases like "Till death do us part" or "As long as we both shall live." Other phrases usually included in the wedding ceremony are "for richer or poorer," "in sickness and in health," and the big one, "for better or for worse." In any case strong promises were made that presupposed that troubled times could be ahead.

Because keeping one's word has long been an indicator of one's character, it is sad to see that so many are trading integrity for what they see as personal gain. The following is a list of the kinds of reasons I have been given for not keeping marriage vows.

1. We just grew apart.
2. He stifled my intellectual growth.

3. She didn't meet my sexual needs and that is very important to me.
4. I lost my respect for him.
5. He was more interested in his hobbies than he was in me.
6. He was moody all the time, always depressed.
7. All we ever did was argue.
8. I'm not sure I ever really loved him in the first place.
9. I just got married to get out of the house, away from my parents.
10. I was just too young to know what I wanted.

In no way do I want to give the impression that the reasons given were not significant problems—they certainly were. Yet all of them are fixable. All these problems and more have been solved to everyone's satisfaction. None are beyond God's ability to heal.

I remember my father teaching me several sayings concerning keeping my word. Here are a few.

1. Thou shalt not lie.
2. The measure of a man is his word.
3. A man's word is his bond.
4. A man's word is all he's really got.
5. If you can keep your word, you can keep your friends.
6. Don't make a promise you can't keep.

I don't remember my father ever making a promise he didn't keep. At his funeral he was eulogized as a man of his word. He stood by my mother for better or for worse. She developed significant medical problems that made her very depressed. She was alcoholic and drug dependent. She attempted suicide several times and during the last two years before his death he was forced to institutionalize her on several occasions. He visited her with regularity and showed kindness and affection during the entire ordeal. It was unbearably expensive, inconvenient, and lonely, but he never complained. You see he was a for-better-or-for-worse man, and he accepted and played the hand he had been dealt.

My father left me with a legacy. His example was an extraordinary gift of teaching on the subject of promise keeping. He will always have in abundance, my respect, admiration, and love. I will consider myself a successful man if my children remember me so.

3. *"God hates hands that shed innocent blood"* (Prov. 6:17). Every divorce devastates innocent by-standers. We have said enough concerning the children, but there is a larger circle. What about friends? Friends are among the ones that pick up the pieces. They listen for countless hours to the pain that some-one has caused, and they offer support. Sometimes they support with child care, sometimes financially. Often they just hurt because there will be a void in their lives. They used to know Bill and Susan, but Susan ran off with her boss. Bill doesn't come around much anymore. He started feeling as though he was a third wheel and found a group of singles with whom to associate. So the friends make new friends, but they remember the good times with Bill and Susan

and are forced to realize there won't be any more. It hurts, but that's the way it is.

Parents of children who divorce suffer also. They pick up pieces too. They may find themselves with a grown child and grandchildren moving in again. They really can't afford to subsidize the divorce, but when you are parents you have to sacrifice. You may not see your grandchildren as much as you used to or more than you want to, but it's almost certain that the new arrangements will be considerably more awkward than the former. When your children remarry things will be even more confused as additional stepgrandparents are added to the list of people whose feelings must be considered during holidays and special days. There is always the shedding of innocent blood.

4. *"God hates a heart that devises wicked plans"* (Prov. 6:18). The thought here is the question of premeditation. All divorces are premeditated by at least one of the parties. I have lived forty-three years on this earth and have yet to see or hear of an accidental divorce. It is usually planned over a long period of time. There are times when people think in terms of ten or more years—when the children grow up. Some take time to manipulate funds so the divorce will work to their advantage. Some wait till their female mates establish higher incomes so spousal support will be lower. Sometimes the women refuse to become employed so spousal support will be higher. Some wait for lovers to divorce their mates before stepping out of their marriage. How many

marriages could be solved if people put this kind of thinking into solving their marital problems? If He hates premeditated evil, He would love it when people premeditate good.

5. *"God hates feet that run rapidly to evil"* (Prov. 6:18). There is a danger that speakers and writers often face of exaggeration. We may try to prove a point at any cost and are often guilty of spending far too much time forcing round pegs into square holes. It's at this point that I honestly feel that I must say that this verse may not always be applicable to a divorce situation.

Norm Wright once shared in a seminar a cogent statement concerning the posture that two people strike just before they divorce. He said, "Divorce occurs when two people lie exhausted at the base of a wall of indifference which they have erected and are unable and unwilling to try to climb." It takes a long time to build such a wall.

There are facts that are often present that do impact a divorce. Between 80 and 85 percent of the time there is a third party lurking somewhere in the shadows of a divorce. This makes a reconciliation absolutely impossible. Only 15 percent of marriages affected by a third-party involvement stay together five years following disclosure. Although extramarital affairs can never be justified, they often have an explanation. A neglected mate is often a prime candidate for an affair, and the mate who did the neglecting should be willing to extend grace when this has been the case.

It is also sad but true that 45 percent of females and 55 percent of males have extramarital affairs during a ten-year marriage. One affair does not indicate a pattern, and in our society, which is pleasure oriented without self-control, it would be unrealistic to think that divorce is always the best course of action. There is so much at stake.

It is also fair to say that in some unusual cases people wait far too long to seek separation or divorce. Those cases involve physical abuse to children or a mate or multiple cases of infidelity. The turnaround or rate of cure for either problem is dismally low. Asking someone to wait for a miracle would be unwise counsel. If you're a woman and you've been hit, my counsel is throw in the towel. Don't hang around for a second round. Separate and force your mate to seek professional counsel. A second occasion of abuse would, in my estimation, be more than grounds for divorce unless you believe our God supports wife abuse. (God forbid!) The term mental abuse is hard to get a handle on. It is my experience that mental abuse is always present in a deteriorated relationship. That can be rehabilitated.

In cases where divorce is permissible but not mandated, it is best to hold out as long as you can without doing permanent damage to yourself or to your children. Seek wise objective counsel that will help you to understand your options and take the hard road as often as possible. The bottom line is that when everything is said and done you will be sure in your heart that there is nothing left for you to do, no stone left unturned. In a society geared for the easy fix and the path of least resistance, it is hard to keep people from bailing out too soon.

6. *"God hates false witnesses who utter lies"* (Prov. 6:19). We have already seen that God hates a lying tongue. That had to do with the breaking of promises by one or both of the marriage partners. False witnesses are those who are asked to lie on behalf of one of the divorcing partners, to give them an advantage, usually concerning child custody.

Think back to the story of my friend in chapter five. I have known him for twenty-one years. We know each other as well as any two people can and there isn't much that has not been shared. Nothing has been withheld—somethings perhaps forgotten. As I shared before, I was best man at his wedding. So it was devastating when I learned that he was being divorced by his wife of thirteen years. He wept when we first talked about it. I had never seen him weep before, and it disturbed me to see him in such pain. He was hunched over, nearly in a fetal position, and he rocked back and forth as he recounted the rejection he had experienced. Before the divorce proclamation was placed in his hands he had participated in years of marital counseling to no avail. The deterioration continued like a spreading cancer and the day came when his wife would no longer put forth the effort to work on the marriage. Zest for life had been his greatest asset. "How long does it hurt?" he asked, as tears progressed past his cheeks and fell softly on our sofa.

In twenty-one years I have never known him to be unkind to anyone. He is supportive and generous, helping others sacrificially and never really expecting anything in return. He is enthusiastic, positive, and encouraging to be around. Everyone who knows him likes him, and he is brimming with integrity. He is a mature and model Christian. All this is to say that this is not the man that his wife pictured through the testimony of her friends and parents. First her parents wrote that the children should be awarded to their daughter because he was a reckless driver. He has had no traffic violations at all. One of his wife's friends was encouraged to write that he was permissive and encouraged his children to watch sexually explicit movies on their home television. He would die first. Her friends credited her with helping with the children's homework when in fact he was their helper. He was accused of mental abuse and being too unstable to be the primary influence with the children. The later psychological testing vindicated him, and he was awarded the majority of the custody of the children. His wife even enlisted the testimony of a minister in a local church to recommend that she was the more fit of the two to care for the children. He did this without ever meeting my friend.

Most divorces turn out this way. They are filled with false witnesses uttering lies. We have a father attending our group who is falsely accused of molesting his children. Mates accuse mates of hiding assets or cheating them out of possessions that don't exist. A common practice is to accuse a mate of having a drug or alcohol problem to create doubt as to their fitness.

The truth is that there is hardly a lie that hasn't been uttered during the divorce process.

7. *"God hates one who spreads strife among brothers"* (Prov. 6:19). Divorce forces friends to take sides. On more than one occasion in churches I have served there were times that a couple would divorce in a church fellowship. Each partner would rally support for their position. There were times when pastors were brought in to bring order and peace to Sunday morning fellowship groups. I served a church where the staff was divided over whether it was any of the church's business to have an opinion at all even though the husband was begging for help to preserve his family. Divorce always spreads strife.

Just as our faith is hard work at times and we sometimes have to pay a high price for it, it is also true that marriage is hard work. A great marriage is a full-time job. When Carol and I were first married, our pastor, Bernard Travaille, shared a great truth in a Sunday morning sermon. "Marriage is a garden. If you fail to take care of it, it will become a jungle, and jungles are dangerous places to live."

Being obedient to God is costly. It's hard work to maintain a good marriage and hard work to fix one that's broken, but it's worth it and it's expected. Faith demands personal sacrifice.

8. *"God hates it when sacrifices are burned to other gods"* (Jer. 44:4–5). God demands first place in our lives, and that means our obedience. Divorce is contrary to God's intention that marriage is a lifelong

commitment. Many states have no-fault divorce laws, but I have never heard a divorce described where someone was not guilty of breaking her or his word in some way.

9. *"I reject your festivals, nor do I delight in your solemn assembles"* (Amos 5:21). God hates hypocrisy. When we say that Jesus is Lord that means we give Him authority over our lives. If we divorce without just cause, we are stating that our personal happiness is more important than His will. Then we are not living what we say we believe. That's hypocrisy.

10. *God hates garments covered with wrong; namely, immorality.* As mentioned before, in 80 percent of the divorces we've studied there was an affair helping to precipitate it.

11. *God loved Jacob, but He hated Esau* (Mal. 1:1–2). Esau didn't regard God's blessing or the things of God important. He equated them as having no more value than a pot of stew. It is clear that God values marriage, and it is important to Him that we do also. Underlying the alarming increase in divorce is the thought that we have a right to be happy. Even our Constitution guarantees us the rights to life, liberty, and the pursuit of happiness. C. S. Lewis wrote an article for the *Saturday Evening Post* in December 1962 just before he died. It was entitled, "We Have No 'Right to Happiness.'" In it he comments on the intentions of the framers of the Constitution: "What

did the writers of the august declaration mean? It is quite certain what they did not mean. They did not mean that man was entitled to pursue happiness by any and every means—including, say, murder, rape, robbery, treason, and fraud. . . . No society could be built on that basis."

Lewis goes on to point out that they intended happiness to be pursued through lawful means. No one would argue that one person could take the life of another because that person's existence made her or him unhappy. Neither could we justify theft on the basis that the thief could not be happy without the possession of an article of great value. We clearly recognize that "Thou shalt not kill" and "Thou shalt not steal" are divine decrees.

"What we have attempted to do is isolate sexual happiness," Lewis says, "and make God's proclamations on morality exceptions." The truth is our happiness cannot be obtained if it means forsaking His will. Forsaking His will always brings sorrow.

I asked my single parent fellowship to fill out a survey that included forty-three questions dealing with the subject of their divorces. The group is made up of about five hundred people who we see during a month. From this point on we will occasionally offer the results of the survey for you to think about. Everyone who took the survey is an authority on the subject. We asked them the following question. "In one sentence or paragraph why do you think God hates divorce?" Their answers were:

1. It's never over for anyone completely.
2. It devastates families.
3. He sees in graphic detail our losses and pain.
4. It makes people wonder if being a Christian makes any difference.
5. It produces so much pain and damage to the people involved. It does anything but demonstrate His glory.
6. It breaks up families for generations to come.
7. It breaks a sacred commitment and everyone involved gets hurt.
8. Children are denied a normal childhood.
9. He knows and feels our total despair and emptiness. His heart of love grieves for His children.
10. Divorce leaves a family in a state of insecurity and confusion.
11. Because of the long-term harmful effects it has on all of us.
12. Raising children separately is just not the way He intended it.
13. The children's loyalties are torn between the two people they love most.
14. God designed the family as a unit, anything less doesn't work.

What do you think? I think God *hates* divorce.

9

For Those Who Initiate Divorce

AT FORTY-THREE YEARS OF AGE I'm old enough to
look back at more past than I have future. G. W. F.
Hegel, the German philosopher, once stated, "The
only thing that we have learned from history is that
we have learned nothing from history." That may be
more true than it is false, but I have learned from my
own mistakes and also from the mistakes of others.
This chapter contains two case studies that reflect
what happens to the initiators of divorce. Try to listen
to them because these could likely be your story if you
make the wrong decision.

KIM AND JOHN AND BRAD AND JULIE

Kim and John had been married for ten years. If
you had asked John about their marriage he would

have told you, "It has its problems, but it's probably better than most." He wasn't worried about his own position in the marriage, but he was aware that Kim was somehow dissatisfied. He didn't really know how to satisfy her. He just hoped that she would get used to the way things were. His whole family background declared that people stayed married—happy or not. Divorce was out of the question. He didn't want one and would never have guessed that Kim would want a divorce either.

Kim was far more in touch with her feelings. She knew that she was in trouble. She couldn't survive many more gray mornings and found herself fantasizing that Prince Charmings were coming to rescue her from her mundane existence. She had found herself attracted to other men but never let them know, nor did she let John know the jeopardy their marriage faced. The more time that passed, the easier it became to visualize and accept the dissolution of their marriage.

Then the worst possible thing happened. John and Kim became best friends with Brad and Julie. Brad was an enormously successful business man, and Julie was his dutiful and dependent wife. Kim became very attracted to Brad and fantasized a Cinderella-like existence with him. If only they had a way of coming together. . . . Kim experienced a fair amount of guilt for her feelings and shared them with her husband John. She even suggested that they move to the East Coast or change churches so the temptation might be removed. John heard what she was saying, but he failed to comprehend just how caught up in her fantasy she had become. He told her that they would just have to face the problem head on. They could never run away from Brad. Deep down John never believed that Brad could betray him. Although he was hurt that his wife was attracted to his best friend, he thought that with time she would get over it.

Brad was as unhappy in his situation as Kim was with hers. He had been seeking relief from his boredom by having out-of-town affairs. Although they were exciting, they didn't fill the void. Like Kim, he had stayed with his marriage because of their children. He had a dwindling Christian faith and had more or less justified his affairs as the better alternative to divorce. The effect, however, was that he was becoming more predisposed to divorce than ever. The bonds were unraveling.

During some unfortunate, unguarded moment, Brad revealed to Kim that he was desperately unhappily married and was grieved that life had dealt him such a boring hand. This was just what Kim had hoped for. She now had the opportunity to live out her fantasy. She quickly revealed that she had the same feelings about her life and risked rejection by confessing her fantasies for Brad. Brad confessed that he had deep feelings for Kim and the affair was launched.

In retrospect, Kim freely admitted that the relationship was based on lust rather than love, but the thrill was back into her existence and there seemed to be no turning back. The exhilaration convinced her that any sacrifice was worth pursuing the relationship.

When the relationship became public there was an

endless stream of pastors and friends who took the time to express their feelings. They told her that she was making a horrible mistake. Letters, phone calls, and visits were endured, but her course was set. She patiently tolerated all the well-meaning intentions of her friends, justifying herself when she thought she could with the line that, "I need to do this in order to be happy." She freely admitted that she was wrong but shared, "God will forgive me for this in time, and whatever He might do to me, it will be worth it."

Kim and Brad both initiated divorce proceedings against their broken-hearted mates who would gladly have forgiven them of all their indiscretions. Kim and John's divorce went through fairly smoothly, but Brad and Julie went to war. It was a $50,000 process and dragged on for three years.

John seemed to be facing problems on every front. His job was phased out in northern California, and he was moved to a desert community in southern California. He had lost his wife, his children (except on weekends and holidays), and his support group. Even his family, who lived in southern California, were just far enough to make talking to them a bit expensive. John's world caved in on him.

From John's perspective, he was experiencing a royal injustice—he called it "the shaft." Kim was driving a Mercedes, eating out at the finest restaurants, a member of a wine-tasting club and a country club, and she was traveling extensively all over the world. He was stuck in a lackluster setting, more alone than he had ever been in his life. From John's perspective, Kim had it made. She had everything anyone could ever want, and her life was all hearts and flowers.

Yet looks are often deceiving. Despite the outward trappings, Kim was experiencing a misery she had never imagined. For more than a year after the divorce she had the feeling that God had left her for good. She never felt His presence and carried with her a gnawing guilt that ate at her soul like a cancer. She knew no peace and there was a constant sense of condemnation. She had been told that she had committed a type of unforgivable sin. Because she had married her lover, they would be living in adultery for the rest of their life. That's the way she felt; there was no way back.

She said to me, "Gary, you know how I felt? It was like when you walk out on a bright sunshiny day, but you cannot see the sun. It was like I was enveloped in my own private night. The worst part of it was that I took it wherever I went. It was just like I had always pictured hell to be.

"I tried to read Scripture, but a terrible feeling came over me whenever I did. I attended all sorts of Christian gatherings, always looking for a way back, but what I heard always made me feel worse.

"I could see what the divorce was doing to my two boys. They were miserable. The youngest cried a lot because he missed his father, and I could also see grief in my oldest. It was tearing them apart, and because I was remarried there was no way to undo the harm that I had done. It was obvious that the boys resented their stepfather and would never accept him. I didn't feel close to Brad's children. There was always tension in our home. I have come to accept that things will always be like this. We will never know a close-knit family again. It's just the way it is with stepfamilies.

"Since Brad and I came into the marriage as adulterers, we have always wondered whether the other would remain faithful. It is a haunting feeling that comes and goes, but it never goes for very long. I am especially uneasy when he goes on business trips, and he is uneasy when we are socializing with good-looking married men. Insecurity is not a good foundation for a remarriage.

"We lost nearly all our close friends, so we had to start all over again. I hated to see people who had known me as John's wife and avoided them at all costs. This was a great sadness because we really had some special friends. It was lonely for a long time. I still feel shame when I see friends that know what I did. It just isn't something about which you can ever be proud."

I asked Kim if it was worth it? She quickly answered, "It's never worth it to cross God."

I also asked her if she thought she had found what she was looking for when she left John. She paused for a long time and said with a definite air of sadness in her voice, "I don't know."

Brad and Kim will never be proud or feel good about what they did, but they have tried to take the steps left open to them to salvage as much of their integrity as possible. Brad wrote a letter to John ten years after the divorce, and John responded. Notice the regret and pain reflected in these letters and ask yourself, "Wouldn't it be best never to get yourself into this mess in the first place?"

Brad's Letter

Dear John,

I realize too many years have passed by, nonetheless, I feel I must deal in whatever way I can with the wrong I have done you and the hurt and pain I brought into your life.

It's difficult for me now to comprehend how I could have hurt so many people including a wife who loved me, my children, and my best friend—passion can really be blinding. Kim and I have carried a lot of guilt. We feel the Lord, in His compassion, has forgiven us, but there will always be scars as reminders. We are especially thankful that the kids have come through as well as they have, but we realize there are many tough years ahead. They will need our prayers and tender guidance.

Anyway, old friend, I wanted to write this letter to sincerely apologize to you for the horrible wrong I committed. There are no excuses—you were always a good and caring friend. I just let myself get caught up and would not put on the brakes. Frankly, I don't know if I could bring myself to offer forgiveness if the situation were reversed, but I'm led to ask forgiveness from you.

Sincerely,
Brad

John's Letter

Dear Brad,

It's been about four months since I received your letter, and I need to respond. I didn't answer sooner because, frankly, I really never expected an apology from you and had no clue as to how to reply.

First things first—you are and have been forgiven by me for about two years.

It took that long for the Lord to bring me to the place where I could see that my hatred for you and what you did was destroying my life. At that point, because God commanded it and because it was consuming me, I gave in and forgave. Since then my life has improved.

What your letter has done has caused me to reflect on the past ten years. The two things that stand out the most are the loss of my boys and being betrayed.

The times you now take for granted with Dale and Eric are moments that were mine. The good, the bad, the happy, and the sad are all times that should have been mine; I'll never retrieve that time and neither will my sons.

Betrayal is hard to recover from. The two people I trusted and loved the most hurt me. For some reason, Brad, I have always felt you were more responsible than Kim for the circumstances. She tried to warn me and I never heard it—but our friendship was somehow special, and I put far too much faith in it and never saw what was going on. You really blindsided me. Until recently I have had a very hard time getting close to another male.

This letter has turned out to be much more personal than I thought it would be. There was a long period when I was sure I would never recover, but let me tell you what God has done. I have been blessed far beyond what I ever could have hoped for—my relationship with Ellen is quite special—it's what I always pictured marriage being. Kurt is super [John and Ellen's son]. Through him, God is giving me back the years I missed with Dale and Eric. Also the relationship I have with Dale and Eric is warm, loving, and extremely close.

Brad, thank you for your letter. I know it was hard for you to write, and I appreciate it.

Asking my forgiveness is probably the easiest part of the process. Seeing the results of your actions has got to be the tough part. There was a long time my fondest desire was to see you burn in hell for what you did. It's taken the Lord a long time to bring us both around—but He has and I no longer feel ill will toward you. In fact, I often miss our friendship. I pray the Lord will bless you and give you peace of mind.

John

GREENER GRASSES

Curt and Marie were the all-American couple achieving the American dream. Curt was a handsome USC graduate, and Marie was the product of an elite Eastern finishing school. Curt was the vice president of a successful bank and had provided a more-than-comfortable existence for his family. They were well on their way to financial security, having a healthy savings account and two income properties that were increasing in value at a phenomenal rate.

Their children were darling—a girl, six, and a boy, three. Everyone loved Curt and Marie; you couldn't help it. They were perhaps the most admired couple in our church. They were actively involved with the youth work, and many high schoolers flocked to their home to spend time with them. They were fun, up to date, and had the gift of hospitality. They were winners by all standards of measurement, and everyone wanted to be just like them, until tragedy struck their home.

Their three-year-old son, Andrew, was diagnosed as having a deadly cancerous tumor growing next to his brain. Curt and Marie responded with courage and faith. Both were an inspiration to everyone. Andrew went through what proved to be a very successful surgery, but only time would prove that he was healed beyond a shadow of a doubt. The surgery was followed by radiation therapy, and Andrew lost his bushy head of silky brown hair. There was no guarantee that the cancer would not return, and it was almost certain that the radiation would affect his growth. He would most probably be stunted.

Curt and Marie seemed towers of strength, comforting others as often as they themselves were comforted. As time passed, it seemed that everyone's prayers for Andrew were answered. One year passed, then two, and there was no sign of new cancer.

By all appearances their storm had passed, or so we thought. Curt and Marie were our very close friends, and no one was more surprised than Carol and I when Curt showed up on our front doorstep and asked to come in. He was pale, and his expression was an incredible mixture of sorrow, humiliation, confusion, and anger.

"Marie has filed for divorce and she's asked me to leave our home," Curt said.

"What happened?" I asked in disbelief.

"I don't know, except she's found another man. Am

I going crazy? I didn't even know that we had a problem, and all of a sudden I'm locked out of my own house, and I can't even see my own children when I want to."

"Well, if you're going crazy, then we all are. None of us saw this coming, Curt." Carol and I were living in a home with a large guest room with its own adjoining bathroom. We could see how broken Curt was and how necessary it was that someone stand by him, so we invited him to stay with us until he felt he needed to be on his own.

Their story began to emerge as the days passed. Something in Marie must have snapped as she walked through the terrifying tunnel of her son's cancer, and she sought relief from her own pain through the diversion of an affair. She became convinced that her own marriage was unfulfilling, and that she owed it to herself to seek a more exciting future. All of her pursuit was in secret. She never told even her closest friends what she was doing. What she was doing was hunting, and when she found what she thought she was looking for, she simply seduced her prey and claimed it for herself. Her prey was also married and had two children.

Most of Marie's close friends went to her and begged her not to continue with her plans to divorce Curt. She would not listen, insisting that she had found the man of her dreams and that she wasn't about to give him up. He was deeper than Curt, more intellectually stimulating. He had an appreciation for the finer things in life: good books, the theater, the ballet. He was gentle and sensitive, and he understood her deepest needs. He was also a finer sex partner.

Curt began to adjust to the idea that he was being divorced, but he needed in the worst way to know why he was being divorced. Marie was faithful at writing in her diary and Curt knew that if he could obtain it, he would be able to determine just why all this was happening to him.

He waited one morning for her to leave the family residence, and he entered quickly, easily finding the diary. He took it to his office and photocopied it. He returned it to its secret place before Marie returned home. Then he read the copy to find his answers.

It was all there. He read her confessions that she was losing her love for him. She gave no particular reason beyond her own feeling that he was no longer her intellectual equal. She pictured him as an insensitive jock, incapable of satisfying her deeper needs. She even recorded that she felt it was time to "trade upwards" in mates.

She recorded the day that she found her ideal man. He was the manager of a local gourmet market, and she determined to seduce him after an engaging conversation in the deli section of his market. The diary recorded the seduction and every secret and sordid move they made over an incredible six-month period. She did acknowledge some remorse over leaving Curt because he really was a nice guy. But the divorce would be to her best interest and that of the children also, she thought.

During the first trial following a thorough investigation, Curt, to his amazement and great joy, was awarded custody of the children. His joy, however, was dashed during the appeal by a judge who didn't read the child service's recommendations and pronounced his judgments on the basis that "children need a mother."

I'll never forget the night following the trial. Curt, Carol, and I sat in our den and relived the decision over and over. We asked questions like "How does a man like that become a judge?" "Children need a father, too. Can't he see that?" We could see that Curt was dying inside, and there wasn't anything that we could do to make it stop hurting. He buried his head in his hands and wept. In between sobs, he lamented that his dream was ended. All that he had worked for, his family and his home, were down the tubes. It would never be the same. As he rose to go home, his shoulders were bent as though he were carrying the weight of the world. He looked back and shrugged as he choked back a sob. As he closed the door, I was sure that he would have one of those never-ending sleepless nights.

My frustration could never have equalled his, but I felt as if I were going to burst with anger. Until that day I had believed in justice, and since then I have been a skeptic. I'm of course speaking of earthly justice. It now seemed like justice could be equated with nothing more than the roll of the dice. The judge in the first trial had read the material, and if you were to get him, something fair might happen. If you drew the second judge, you were in trouble. Nothing more than the luck of the draw. As a Christian, I was sure that God was in the situation, and for those that loved Him there would be justice someday. But someday didn't seem soon enough. I ached as my close friend cried softly into the early morning hours.

I felt angry; angry at Marie, at her lover, at a capricious judge, and angry with God for allowing this to happen. I thought through all the events that had brought all the players to this moment and tried to sort out why I was feeling the way that I did. I grabbed my guitar and fumbled through a few haunting melodies and wrote this song. It expressed much of what Curt was feeling and included a lot of what I was feeling that night also.

Part-Time Dad

Happy times, my memory's fading.
Children's laughter has gone astray.
Locked alone in life's dark shading,
Longing for a sun-shiny day.

Gray the dawn my life is silent,
Gone the dreams for which I've paid.
Mind is spinning, spirit's joy spent,
Nursing wounds this strife has made.

Breaking bonds that God has joined forever,
Killing love He'd given by His grace.
The children cry, they feel the pain forever,
Touching scars time never will erase.

Saturday, here come the children,
Growing tall and looking grand.
Do you want some chocolate candy?
Want to go to Disneyland?
Does your mother still embrace you?
Does the new man tuck you in?

Read you stories? get you band-aids?
Gee, I've missed you, how you been?

Breaking bonds that God has joined forever,
Killing love He'd given by His grace.
The children cry, they feel the pain forever,
Touching scars time never will erase.

Sunday's here, was good to see you.
Guess it's time to take you home.
Did I say, I have a girlfriend?
Keep you posted, let you know.
Give a hug and know I love you.
Part-time father's not my style.
Mind your mom, be good at school.
See you in a little while.

Breaking bonds that God has joined forever,
Killing love He'd given by His grace.
The children cry, they feel the pain forever,
Touching scars time never will erase.

Marie married her lover, but none of what she had fantasized ever came to pass. It turned out that she had overlooked some very important considerations. She had discounted the fact that her new husband had a history of mental illness. She had been warned, but she chose to believe that his problems were all in the past and he would not be violent to her as he had been with his first two wives. She chose to believe that his tendency to drink too much was really not significant. But it turned out to be.

He came very close to killing her, and she divorced him after just two years of marriage. Justice prevailed, but it brought not one ounce of the satisfaction for which I had once longed. Marie had been crushed under the weight of her own bad choices, and there was no way back for her or her children. She was a tragedy, and my compassion brought me to pity. She wanted her family back, but Curt had met an absolute Cinderella and had the good sense to marry her before anyone else snapped her up. There was no way to undo the damage that she had done, and she chose to continue her search for happiness in all the wrong places.

Ten years have passed since these events, and you might appreciate an update on the parties involved in this story. Curt is very happily married to Cindy and is living in a woodsy rural community in northern California. They have an addition, Josh, a strong-willed, extremely active little guy who keeps them busier than either of them would like to be. Curt is very happy in his career and has helped found a successful church in their thriving community.

I honestly wish that I could tell you that Marie is doing fine and portray a happy ending, but it wouldn't be the truth. Marie is simply living with a man unhappily. They are not married, nor are they planning to be married. Their relationship, as described by Marie's daughter, is "Two people sitting around, drinking beer, and yelling at each other." Their daughter Susan has perhaps suffered the most from the divorce. She is severely bulimic and is in counseling four days out of the week. Andrew was spared a recurrence of cancer and attained a height of five feet. He is well adjusted, considering the circumstances, and has a fairly positive outlook on life.

I wrote a song concerning Marie. It was written before her world caved in and while I was still very angry about the hurt that she had caused. Still it expresses some truths concerning people who insist on abandoning their values and convictions about vows and truth and faithfulness and the things that really matter.

Little Moth

Little moth is flying to the flame
Tattered wings will soon proclaim her shame.
For she thought she'd found a brighter light,
Than the stars that guide her through the night.

Fallen to the ground now never more to lift your
Wings in flight. Lift your wings in flight.

Little moth is filled with fear and pain.
Looking for another moth to blame.
Was it not your eyes that claimed this light,
And your wings that brought you there in flight.

Fallen to the ground now never more to lift your
Wings in flight. Lift your wings in flight.

Little moth there's no more time to learn.
Your wings are gone and you have lost your turn.
Should-of-beens won't alter yesterday.
You'd been warned, there's nothing more to say.

Fallen to the ground now never more to lift your
Wings in flight. Lift your wings in flight.

WHY, DAD?

There are several consequences of divorce for those who choose to initiate it. The one that strikes me as most important is that of having missed God's best. I have interviewed several people who were initiators and all of them reflected that they had not improved their life situations through divorce. They all shared the common perception that they would, but none of them did. I fully realize that there are probably some who feel better divorced or remarried, but I assure you that the vast majority don't, and studies support this statement. There are many reasons. Some are mentioned in the stories and some aren't. Let me list them.

1. If you are a Christian, you are likely to carry with you for the rest of your life the feeling that you took a wrong turn and that God's best will never again be available to you.
2. You will be plagued with a nagging sense of guilt and remorse for the emotional damage that you caused. It will be heightened as you see the effects that it has on your children or your former spouse, who, when everything has been said and done, didn't really deserve to be set aside.
3. Statistics show that second marriages have a 70–75 percent rate of failure. You may be confronted with the reality that you may have been more of a problem in your first marriage than you care to admit. Third marriages have a more than 85 percent rate of failure. Your chances of finding happiness through remarriage will begin to seem unlikely.
4. If your situation involved infidelity, you will always wonder whether you or your new mate

will be faithful. If you haven't been faithful and they haven't, what's to say that either of you will be different in the future.

5. You will find that it will be some years before the people who took you seriously previously will again take you seriously. Not only will self-respect be a problem, but disrespect will be a problem. Trust is the basis of any relationship. Because you violated that trust, you will be on the outside looking in when matters concerning things of lasting value are handled between close friends or family members. The loss of trust from your own children is a given in cases where you have broken your promises. You will find that a bitter pill to swallow, but that is what will happen.

Consider the following letter from a distraught son expressing his deepest feelings to his father who had betrayed the family. I have seen many of these kinds of letters in the last few years, but I think this one best expresses the loss of respect that occurs when a parent violates her or his marriage vows. The son's feelings are clear. Try to read between the lines to determine the son's unstated request.

Bret's Letter

Dad,

It is hard to write this because I know this whole thing hurts, at least it does me. First, I want to tell you that I love you and that we all do. Janie and I did not make the initial decision to leave, but we have made that decision now with mom. I know that you have not really worked at your marriage, let alone your relationship with Janie and me. I mean you never really poured yourself into me—I don't really know you. I have never cried with you or known any of your real feelings. You always seemed to cover them up with callousness or bitterness toward the negative side of something. Sometimes I wonder if you hold any sentiment or any ruth (you are ruthless). One thing I do know, Dad, is that I still want to know you more because I love you and need you—I want us to be close and best friends as father and son.

I think you should remember that marriage is something very sacred to God—it is representative of Jesus Christ and the church, and, yes, this is even something that God has given us in order to learn "government" and how to be rulers with Him. How are you at "family politics?" I also remind you, Dad, that you told me and some of your books on communism have also said that one serious tool used by communism in its struggle to uproot this country is to break down the family structure. It doesn't necessarily happen in the first few generations, but later on, because more and more people don't have a good example of a right marriage—you've seen it in your own son's marriage. Was it because he forgot or chose to discard a good example he had in you?

I want to point out one more thing, with love, Dad. You have been dishonest financially—I need not explain. You have shown hatred and bitterness toward brothers in Christ instead of forgiveness and love. Would you be found guilty if you were accused of being a Christian—you have destroyed the proof that God has given. "They will know we are Christians by our love." You have not been honest; you have no integrity, forgiveness, and love. How can God use someone who blatantly lives against the fundamentals that God says we need (1 Corinthians 13)? You always told me in basketball, "never forget the fundamentals," "go up with two hands, one to lay the ball up and the other to get the foul"—Dad, you're making a lot of "one-handed lay-ups."

You are a mastermind at politics, just the "nuts and bolts" of the whole system, but that is useless if you lose sight of "Why?"—to glorify God! I am afraid, Dad, that politics is starting to beat you instead of you being the super conqueror in Christ that you are and overcoming it. I know you think I am not committed like other Christians, but you're wrong—I see the need too and know God is going to use me there, but I can't do it with you. You see—I need someone who will help lift me up and whom I can lift up, who will remind me of the fundamentals and about whom all that ultimately counts is our relationship with our Lord. I can't have someone who cuts on other Christians constantly, who doesn't know when to draw the line between work and quality time for their relationships.

Dad, I think this whole thing is up to you now—you can make this thing as impermanent and short and productive as you want (and we want) or you can drag it out. I pray that you'll want to keep us a family and do what is right in God's sight. It would be good to think, also, of the effect that your reaction will have on Bill, Sue, and Trix, other relatives, and even friends. God could use it to help strengthen these people and their relationships.

I don't want you to feel super judged. We realize we
have faults that make us hard to live with, but we just
want to all work together to be closer. People need
the Lord, but they need people too—God shows Himself through His children. I love you so much, Dad,
and I hope this gets over soon so we can go on to a
better relationship.

From my heart,
Bret

I know the boy who wrote this letter, and I know
how painful it was for him to write it. As you move
through the letter you can feel Bret's heart breaking. I
could feel the frustration of a son who could not understand why his father would choose to set a course
that would destroy the family. Bret wanted so badly to
be close to his father, but he saw that his father was
the kind of man who made that difficult. Bret saw his
father's life as a contradiction to what he had always
taught him. Bret had lost his respect for his father and
was now finding himself in the awkward position of
trying to set his father straight. You might question
whether or not a son should be saying the kind of
things that Bret said, but try to look beyond that to
the hurt that caused him to say them. Bret's last
words in the letter still echo in my mind, "I love you
so much, Dad, and I hope that this gets over soon so
we can go on to a better relationship."

These kind of feelings go deep. If you are thinking
that children are resilient—they will get over the divorce soon—you simply don't understand children.
For them, their feelings for you will never be the

same, especially if you are the initiator and they know it. Bret was eighteen, and the situation was very clear to him. He understood just what was going on. Your situation may be very different from Bret's or his father's, but some of the elements of what took place in their story will take place in yours. You will see the hurt. You will feel the disrespect.

Can you see how complicated this is all becoming? You may be in a horrible situation, but if there is any way to salvage it, it would be easier than what lies ahead for you if you don't try. The next two chapters will be devoted to those who might want to try just one more time to see if there is a way to make their marriages work. Go ahead and risk reading two more chapters. I have told you the truth about what divorce is like. Now look into reconciliation. We see it work all the time. It would be great for your children and your mate, your friends and extended family, and God will be pleased. He will help you if you honor Him in this way.

10

Nothing's Impossible When God's Involved

VICKY WAS YOUNGER THAN MOST who come into my office for comfort and guidance. She had three little girls, all under five years of age, and she looked tired. Any mother with three children under five looks tired, but she was beyond tired; she was on empty. I could tell she had long ago come to the end of her rope. At best, she was just hanging on. There was a single thread supporting Vicky over an abyss of despair and whatever comes after sanity. She needed encouragement, and I prayed I would be given the special grace to pull her away from the edge. I asked her to tell me her story.

Her first words were, "Pastor, I need help. I'm not sure what to do. I left my husband about a year ago, and he wants to come back. I think I'm supposed to, but I just can't. I can't face it the way it was, but things are getting tough here, and I just don't know what to do next."

"Vicky, what happened, what went wrong? What did your husband do that caused you to leave him?"

A tear fell from her cheek, and she apologized for being so emotional. I assured her that that was the way she should be under her circumstances, and it would be good if she didn't try to hold it in.

She cleared the tears with the back of both hands and summoned the pluck to tell her story. "My husband's name is Brad. He works in the oil fields near Bakersfield, California. We've been married six years. It wasn't so bad the first few years, until we both got into drugs. I think we both knew drugs were wrong, but it kind of got a hold on us.

"Brad made real good money in the oil fields, but our drug bill was pretty heavy, and paying the bills was getting super hard. Brad's personality began to change. When he would come off his cocaine highs, he would become very abusive. He slapped me around on a regular basis and yelled at me all the time. He began running around with other women. Although I knew it was going on, he would always lie about it, so I could never believe that he was telling me the truth about anything. I was four-months pregnant with Shawna (their third child), and one night when he was very enraged I thought he would punch me in the stomach and hurt the baby inside me.

"That was the last straw. I packed my bags and headed for my parents' house. They had a

four-bedroom house, but my three brothers were all
still living at home, and the three girls and I all had
to sleep in one bedroom. My father is an alcoholic,
and it seemed to me that every day when I came
home from work he would tell me what a burden I
was and how he hated having our kids in his home. I
couldn't afford to go anywhere else, and I hated being there. My older brother was drunk most of the
time, and when he would get drunk he would push
me around and slap me.

"I have thought a lot about killing myself lately, but
I don't because of the girls. I just don't know who
would take care of them.

"Just after Shawna was born, my husband Brad
moved in with another woman. But we have talked
on the phone lately, and he tells me he wants to get
back together. I want him back, but not the way he
was. I just don't know what to do. I'm so unhappy."

She was nearly in a fetal position, and she held
herself as she rocked back and forth sobbing.

"Vicky," I said softly, "you're in a tight spot, and
right now things don't look too good. But it's my experience that there is always a way through. You've
come too far to give up now. Let's take one step at a
time. If you take more than that it's too difficult.
First, Brad. He's living with another woman, and as
long as he is, there is no way to put your marriage
back together. As long as a third party is in the picture, nothing can be fixed. You won't trust him, and
he will still depend on her emotionally. So nothing
will happen for the better if you try to work on your
marriage. Because he still has a problem with drugs

and alcohol, chances are he will still be a danger to you and eventually to your children. I'm afraid if you want him back, you're just going to have to wait for him to get his life in order. That may take a long time, and it may never happen. It is very hard for men who have had several affairs to stop, so if you take him back you may see considerably more of this behavior.

"Because you're a new Christian, I need to tell you that you are free to stay and wait to see what happens. Sometimes miracles do happen. You also need to know that you have God's permission to go. Only you will be able to make the decision, but you are not stuck in this horrible situation forever. Don't go back until he has gotten some first-class help with his problem."

We spent the rest of our time talking a bit about reducing the tension levels at her home so that being with her parents would be a little less traumatic. I encouraged her to become more involved with our single parents program and to make friends with those who cared about her deeply. She did all those things. Although things were still rough at home, she showed a great deal of courage and endured this difficult period.

Things did not improve between Vicky and Brad, so she initiated divorce proceedings to secure financial support for herself and her children. She really hadn't wanted to pursue this course, but it seemed the only avenue open to her. Brad came to see her, but he made no headway on getting her to agree to come back to him.

He came on a Tuesday night and asked someone to

go into the single parents meeting to get me out. He had some things he wanted to say to me about the counsel Vicky had received at the church, and he wanted to say it to my face. I met him in our parking lot, and I must confess that I was less than comfortable when our eyes met. He had been drinking, and he looked very angry. Did I say he was large?

"You the pastor who's telling my wife to stay away from me?" he asked with malevolence.

"Are you the husband who pushes your wife around when you're on drugs and who is staying with another woman?" I returned, a bit testy myself. "Listen, Brad. We always recommend that a wife separate from her husband if she gets the kind of treatment you have given her. The way I see it, you're going to lose everything that has real value in your life if you don't get your life in order. You have three darling children and a wife that's a winner, but you won't have them for long unless you wake up. Yes, I'm the pastor that told your wife to stay away, but if you get some help, we'll support the marriage."

We were pretty much nose to nose. For an instant I wasn't feeling too much like a pastor as I remembered Vicky's stories about the times she had been abused. Brad and I stared at each other for several long seconds, and I noticed that his fist was clenched. He threw down his cigarette and stormed off, leaving me wondering if a more loving approach would have been more effective.

As it turned out, Brad did some serious thinking about his life and what was of value. The next day he made an appointment with Buck Buchanan, our pastor of care and concerns. Buck, with a more loving and caring approach, was able to talk Brad into enrolling in a drug rehabilitation program, which proved to be very effective.

Vicky put the divorce on hold, and they began seeing a skilled marriage counselor who was able to help them to understand that their marriage problems had deep and significant roots. Free from the effects of drugs, they were able to make some real progress.

I inadvertently met Brad on the church steps weeks later and had the distinct feeling that I was talking to an entirely different person. The wild eyes were gone, and he looked at peace. He was very friendly and apologized for the way our last meeting had gone. I felt very heartened that things would be working out. Now I could see the person with whom Vicky had first fallen in love. He was really very nice and now able to take responsibility for the damage he had done to his marriage.

After two and a half years of work, Brad and Vicky moved in together. It was anything but smooth sailing at first, and there were times that both of them wondered if everything was going to fall apart. But they kept making good solid moves that would save the day. They both joined a support group designed to help adult children of alcoholics and gained insight into why they did many of the things they did. They joined an adult fellowship at our church and viewed the kind of examples that help a person understand what marriage is supposed to be.

Vicky and Brad are doing great now. Their process has been a sure and steady one, although I would be less than honest if I were to say that it was easy. No reconciliation after a separation or a divorce is easy. Yet by the grace of God it can be accomplished—and in a way that makes the new relationship better than it has ever been before.

Vicky and Brad decided to renew their vows. They did so in a very special way. They planned a lovely wedding. What was most special was looking down at the faces of their darling children, knowing they were being spared the pains that so many other children have had to endure. Buck and I performed the ceremony, and it seemed a most fitting way to say that they were starting over and were going to get it right this time. I shed tears. I think everyone did.

Coincidentally, I ran into Vicky and Brad recently. They were carrying their newest arrival—a handsome newborn who squirmed with delight as his loving father held and kissed him. I could hardly believe the miracle that stood before me. At our first meeting I wouldn't have given them a one-in-a-thousand chance of staying together. But give God an inch, and He'll take a mile if you're willing to go along for the ride.

Brad and Vicky are not the only victory stories that we have to share. There are many. Brad and Vicky's story was a drastic account. I chose to tell it because it included almost every element that makes getting back together difficult. My hope is that if your situation is difficult, you might think, "If they can make it, so can we."

What I have learned is that solving people's marriage problems has more to do with the character of the people than the complexity of their situation. Needless to say, I have seen marriages end over nothing and survive awesome explosions. If you have one ounce of character, you can make it work.

The most selfish man I have ever met confessed that the only objection he had to his marriage was that his wife did not perform to his level of sexual satisfaction. He admitted that she was a princess in every other way. She endured one and a half years of his immoral explorations and even consented to try to be a better sexual partner. Still, he left her and his two darling little girls. He took up residence with his mistress, but she has since kicked him out after becoming fed up with his self-indulgent ways. He still wallows in a jacuzzi full of self-pity. He doesn't have the character for reconciliation.

Most situations are less of a problem to work with than Brad and Vicky's and more typical. Chuck and Nancy had such a situation.

Chuck came to our office one afternoon and asked if there might be a pastor willing to see him. He explained to our receptionist that he had severe marriage problems and needed to talk to someone right away. He had just left his own church where he was told that everyone was otherwise occupied and if he still needed help he would have to come back another day. Chuck was hurting too badly to go back, and left angry when the only request he had ever made for help was turned down. That's why he came to us. I am very thankful that my schedule had opened up that afternoon, so I was free to talk to him.

Chuck slumped in his chair and I could tell he had

been hurt deeply. He sighed and paused as if he didn't know where to begin.

"How can I help you, Chuck?" I asked.

"My wife is divorcing me, and I don't know what to do," he answered.

I asked him to tell me his story. It was a story I had heard before—many times before. That didn't make it any less painful for him, though, and I gave him my full attention.

"Nancy started having an affair several months ago with a man whom she works with. She just moved in with him, and she has filed for a divorce. She says she doesn't love me any more, and I just don't know what to do."

"Chuck, I can't fool you and tell you that everything's going to be all right, but I can tell you that we will stand by you and help you get through this if she chooses to stay with the affair," I said. "If she wanted to come back, would you want her back?"

"I think so," he said with a puzzled look.

"Well, the fact is that affairs usually come to an end. When they do, you sometimes get a window to launch a reconciliation. Chuck, both women and men usually have affairs to punish their mates for some unfulfilled expectation they had for marriage. They usually don't really love the person with whom they are having the affair. They are just using them to punish their mates. They have feelings, but the feelings are usually just sexual feelings, and they wear off. Let me ask you a really painful question. Did Nancy ever share with you that she wished you would be different in a way that would help your marriage?"

"Yes. She wanted me to spend more time at home. I know that I work too much. She also complained that we never did any of the things she liked to do. She wanted me to be romantic."

"I think she was trying to tell you something. You heard her, but you didn't do anything about it. Do you think you were guilty as charged?"

"I know I was. At the time I thought our marriage probably didn't have any more problems than most and I just let things slide."

"Chuck, I appreciate your honesty. Most men wouldn't admit that they were part of the problem. Do you understand that subconsciously she is saying, 'See if you won't love me, I'll find someone who will'?"

Chuck looked down and said, "Do you think she'll ever come back?"

"There is no way to know. She may come back, but it may be too late. You may not want her back when she's ready to come. Affairs often last more than six months, and the average American male doesn't handle that too well. How long do you think you could wait to get a chance to prove to her you could be a loving husband?"

"I don't know. I don't think I could wait six months."

"I'm not sure I could either. Why don't you see how long you can wait and see what happens. In the meantime, we'll keep you going and as happy as you can be under the circumstances. We have a great single parents program here, and they will help you keep it together and even heal while you're waiting to see how this all comes out."

Chuck threw himself into the single parents program and began to show signs that he would be able to be happy no matter what happened.

The divorce settlement was going along very smoothly, and as there were no children of the marriage it seemed their parting would be considerably more peaceful than most. Chuck had accepted the fact of the divorce and was just allowing the calendar dates to march forward until the painful process resolved itself into a final defeat. Then he would gather himself together and get on with life.

One late afternoon, about the time of day that I first met him, he rushed in to tell me that a mutual friend had called him and told him that his wife's affair had ended and that she might still be interested in being married to him.

He blurted out, "What do I do?"

"Whatever you'd like to do," I answered. "Do you still love her? Do you want her back?"

He sputtered and stammered and said, "I don't know. . . . I think so. . . . I didn't think this would happen. . . . What do I do now?"

"I think at this point you should call her and see if there is any truth to the rumor. Find out if she has any interest in working on the marriage. If she does, make an appointment with my secretary and let's see how much of a foundation we have on which to rebuild.

"Before we can work in the marriage, she has to be

sorry for what she has done, and you must be willing
to forgive her for it. If you are unable to forgive and
she is not sorry, we won't get to first base. Once the
hurdle has been crossed, then we must deal with
the problems of the marriage while we are con-
structing new goals and the hope that you can put it
together."

"Do you think we can do it?" he asked sincerely.

"Only if you want to bad enough. A reconciliation
is only a chance to solve the problems of the marriage that have been seriously complicated by an affair and a divorce action. In a little while you will
find out why nations have such a hard time getting
along. But, still and all, God is involved with this
whole process, and He believes in marriage. It will
surely be worth a try."

Chuck indeed confirmed her interest, and she
agreed to come in for an initial talk to explore the pos-
sibilities. I was excited. When they came in for that
all-important first visit, their body language was an
incredible statement as to our beginning point. The
chairs they sat in were flat against a wall next to each
other. The first thing Chuck did was to pull his chair
away from hers, and they both angled them so that
they would be looking slightly away from each other.
There was a good deal of tension in the room, and I
began with small talk to relax both of them.

"Nancy, Chuck," I finally began, "we're here to
explore the possibility of your putting your marriage
back together. It's important for me to see if there is
enough of a foundation to build on, so I am going
to ask you a lot of questions—some very personal.

Please tell me how you really feel and what you believe to be true about your marriage and your present feelings about each other.

"Nancy, I have gotten to know Chuck during the last few months, so if it would be all right, I would like to begin with you. Tell me about your marriage and why you think it was failing. What do you think opened you up to a relationship with another man?"

Nancy looked down at first and spoke very softly, "I didn't feel very loved by Chuck. He worked a lot, and when he was home he was pretty much involved with his hobby, which I don't really care for very much. I think he thought I was nagging him if I ever said anything about it. So I just hoped it would get better, but it never did. We were married seven years, and I was getting more and more unhappy.

"There was this guy at work, and he started paying attention to me, and he made me feel like a lady again. He seemed interested in what I had to say and even made me feel pretty. We started seeing each other privately, and finally we . . . ," she paused.

". . . became intimate," I coached.

She took a quick sidelong glance, and then looked me in the eye and said, "Yes."

"I understand he is out of the picture now. Is that accurate information?" I pursued.

"Yes."

"What happened?"

"I think I realized he was never really in love with me. He got what he wanted and . . . he dropped me."

"If he wanted you back, would you go?"

"No. I know he would never want me for the right reasons."

"Do you want to go back to Chuck?"

"If it's different. I don't want to go back if it's just the same."

"Chuck, you've heard Nancy's description of what your marriage was like. Do you agree with it?" I asked, hoping he would.

"Yes. It was just like that."

"Do you feel that maybe you made a contribution to her desire to find in another relationship what she was missing in yours?"

"Yes, I do."

"Do you think you could change so her needs would be met?"

"Yes, and I want a chance to try."

I turned to Nancy and asked her if she realized how much the affair had hurt Chuck and if she were sorry. Not sorry that it didn't work out, but sorry for what she had done to Chuck. She said that she knew that it had hurt him, but she did not say any more. I tried to explain that a reconciliation needed to begin with two people admitting their contribution to the failure of the marriage. I further explained that the rebuilding of the trust necessary for a reconciliation to occur was predicated on the feeling that both parties were ready to ask forgiveness for what they had done. Nancy nodded but didn't say anything.

I turned to Chuck and asked, "Are you ready to ask Nancy's forgiveness for the neglect and withholding of love that set her up for this affair?"

Chuck nodded and turned to Nancy and said,

"Would you forgive me for not being a very loving husband and give me a chance to make it up to you?"

Nancy began to cry and surprised me by saying, "I don't know if I am ready to do this yet."

I felt it would be wrong to press for any more commitment and simply asked her to think about it during that week. I ended our time with a few stories designed to offer hope, something about rainbows often following rainstorms, and sent them away. I wondered if I would be seeing them the following week.

They made another appointment, and to my surprise, they both kept it. They didn't change the position of the chairs this time, and I considered that perhaps this would be a more profitable time.

"Chuck, I would like to begin with you telling Nancy your feelings during the period of her absence in your life."

Chuck did a wonderful job of describing his loneliness, feelings of abandonment, loss of value, and depression. He mentioned his anger and jealousy, but through it all he was careful hot to judge her or put her down or make her feel like trash. While he was talking, a tear began a hesitant journey down her slightly freckled cheek. It was joined by another, and they fell together to the arm of her chair. When Chuck noticed it, he carefully took her hand in his and squeezed it. When she gained her composure, she asked for forgiveness. She apologized for what she had done, and it was the good kind of apology—free of any attempt to explain or justify or fix blame on anyone but herself.

A reconciliation was launched that day when two

people asked for and obtained forgiveness. They gave each other a new slate on which to write a new story. From that day on they always held hands during the sessions and turned their chairs toward each other, often looking into each other's eyes while they were speaking.

In the process, I discovered that neither of them had ever had any premarital counseling. We enrolled them in our premarital counseling program and had them working through that while we continued to address the issues that had injured their relationship. They obtained a new view of marriage and established clear and achievable goals for their marriage. We set them free to enjoy their marriage and encouraged them to come in if they experienced any difficulties. There were two or three more visits, and then we didn't see them for several weeks.

I ran into them one Sunday morning and was pleased to note that they were still holding hands. Chuck had a big smile when I asked him how it was going. He looked at her with a good deal of love and shared, "We didn't know it could be this good. Guess what . . . Nancy is pregnant! You know, we tried to have a baby before, but nothing ever happened."

"Maybe God knew just when would be the best time. This baby is going to grow up in a very happy family now. Congratulations."

I have continued to see Chuck and Nancy on the grounds of the church, and they still look like newlyweds. They remind me that "with God all things are possible."

Your situation may be difficult—more difficult

than the situations just shared. You may have biblical grounds for divorce. But according to everything I have seen, it would still be in your best interest to consider a reconciliation. Even if it didn't work you would have the knowledge that you did everything possible to maintain this sacred human relationship. For that you will obtain peace of mind and the respect of those who know you best.

Again, if you have been subjected to any kind of physical abuse or your spouse has had multiple affairs, you may require that they receive special help before you make an attempt to return to them. God would not have you chained to a nightmare of those varieties.

If your situation warrants it, give reconciliation a chance. You may not know where to begin, so read the next chapter. It will give you some special hints.

11

Reconciliation

I F YOU HAVE DECIDED that you would be willing to give your marriage another chance, let me give you some direction. First and foremost, you need to know that if it took you a number of years to get into a troubled marriage, it will take a bit of time to get out. Keep in mind that you will be making progress as you work on your problems. So picture your situation getting better and better over a period of months. It will be a two-steps-forward-and-one-step-back situation, so don't be overwhelmed if your recovery is not consistent. Measure your progress by the month, not by the day.

Old, bad habits of thoughtlessness or poor communication are hard to break, and you must give your mate the freedom to fail. If there has been an affair, your mate will need time and freedom to lose her or his feelings for the one with whom they had the affair. Affairs are addictive and often give the lingering illusion of having filled a void. Give yourself time to rebuild trust. That only comes as a new relationship develops in a positive way. A new track record needs to be established. When it is, the feelings of trust will come back. While you are waiting for the feelings to come back, give your mate the benefit of the doubt. There will be doubts and you must fight them or they will wear you down and rob you of the incentive to keep going. If you are a Christian, pray for the strength to do your part and try to stay away from evaluating your mate's efforts. Your mate can't try as hard as you want them to, so you will need to keep your mind on your own efforts, not your mate's.

There may be such a breakdown of communication in your situation that you will find it necessary to get professional help. Professional help is expensive if it involves a licensed marriage and family counselor, but it still may prove to be the best investment that you ever made in your or your children's future. It is hard for me to report this, but my own experience has confirmed that most counselors are not very effective. I am not casting doubt over a whole professional group, rather I am reminding you that as with any profession there are those who are competent and incompetent.

Do you remember how many teachers inspired you to learn? Not many. Do you remember how many pastors sent you away Sunday after Sunday thrilled and anxious to change your world? Not many. The answer to the question, "How many marriage and family counselors are helpful and have a decent percentage of marital turnarounds?" is unfortunately "not many." Does that mean to avoid professional help? Not on your life! I would no sooner recommend that than tell you not to go to school or not to go to church for fear of remaining ignorant or experiencing boredom. What I am telling you is that you should be careful in your choice of counselors.

I am indebted to Kelsey Menehan for her article entitled, "Good Counseling" published by *Today's Christian Woman*. This article is reproduced as Appendix B in this book. It will help you to know how to choose a professional counselor.

You may not be able to afford a marriage counselor, and you may not need one. Although seminary fails to teach marriage counseling as adequately as it teaches theology, there are many pastors to whom God has given the ability to deal with broken human relationships. Some of the same principles that we just discussed are true when applied to choosing pastors also. I must add that you must choose a pastor whose marriage you respect and whose life you respect. Whoever you choose must hold a high view of marriage and an extremely low view of divorce. If your prospective counselor doesn't and your situation is difficult, he or she will give up when the ideas run out. If you lose confidence in your counselor, dump him or her, and look for another until you feel satisfied.

In the final analysis, you will be most responsible for the success or failure of your reconciliation. The finest counsel in the world will have no effect unless you take it. That means that you should do the assignments, read the books, and spend the time to do what your counselor suggests.

The major problem facing you as you approach this reconciliation is your attitude. If you believe that your problems are unresolvable, they will be. In his short twenty-page booklet, *Attitudes,* Chuck Swindoll makes a startling statement: "This may shock you, but I believe the single most important decision I can make on a day-to-day basis is my choice of attitude. It is more important than my past, my education, my bankroll, my successes or failures, fame or pain, what other people think about me or say about me, my circumstances, or my position."

This pamphlet is reprinted as Appendix A in this book. Unfortunately, the pamphlet is not available in bookstores. Additional copies, however, can be ordered from Insight for Living, P.O. Box 4444, Fullerton, Calif. 92634. You will never read twenty more significant, well-written pages.

There are several problem areas that usually need to be addressed when a couple attempts reconciliation. Among them are forgiveness, communication, ability to reconcile, and attitude. The following are books that deal with these topics.

I would suggest two books for you on the topic of forgiveness. If you won't forgive, you won't reconcile. Read Lewis B. Smedes, *Forgive and Forget.* Another book that deals with this subject is David Augsburger's *Caring Enough to Forgive.* Both are excellent books that will help you any time you need to forgive.

The hardest person to forgive is your mate. Mates learn how best to hurt you and hurt you deeply. Hurt progresses to anger. Anger progresses to hatred. Hatred consumes us and colors our life gray, and then black.

We are commanded to love our enemies and to do good to them that despitefully use us. That is an easy scripture to say "Amen" to until someone despitefully uses you. Then it becomes the hardest. We are also reminded that God Himself will not forgive us until we are willing to forgive those who have sinned against us. Forgiveness is in no way an option, it is an obligation to God. It honors Him when we forgive and more so if we forgive our mates.

Forgiveness is the door that opens up the possibility of reconciliation. Once the door is open it becomes important to deal with the problems that led to the breakdown of the marriage. This is where the hard work begins. There is within all of us the felt need of being the innocent party. If we go into a reconciliation thinking it will be successful when our mates admit that the marriage problems were their fault, they were wrong and we were right, we will probably never see two people rejoined. That means that two people must, after forgiveness, admit the possibility that they made a negative contribution to the relationship. That attitude will open us up to the solution phase of the reconciliation. Do not seek to use your counselor or pastor as your vindicator. You may likely win the battle and lose the war.

There are several books that deal with the subject of the restoration of relationships. They deal with forgiveness, communication, attitude, how to fall in love again, and many other relevant topics. Two books that help many to relate better to each other were written by Gary Smalley and Steve Scott. One was written to men, to help them understand their wives' point of view and the other to the wives so they might better understand their husbands. The titles are *If Only He Knew* and *For Better or for Best*. Not only can these books help in a reconciliation situation, but they can help make a good marriage better. Anything by Gary Smalley and John Trent will be helpful in relationship building. Norm Wright is another master when it comes to teaching people to communicate, and I highly recommend his book on communication, *Communication: Key to Your Marriage*. Richard Strauss, a gifted pastor-teacher, has written a terrific book on communication entitled *Getting Along with Each Other*. Anything you read on communication will speed up the process of healing. If you are paying the going rates for professional counseling, you will see the logic in speeding up the process. There are a number of books that are helpful in working through a reconciliation. All of them are worth considering. I would recommend the following list:

Hope for the Separated, by Gary Chapman
Love Life, by Ed Wheat
Try Marriage before Divorce, by James E. Kilgore
Rebonding, by Donald M. Joy
Rekindled, by Pat Williams and Jill Williams

If finances have played a major role in your broken relationship, then consider reading Ron Blue's right-on book, *Master Your Money*. It might be very helpful if you are willing to adopt his principles.

It is my theory that most marriages that fail are crushed under the weight of unfulfilled expectations. Sometimes the expectations are reasonable and sometimes they are not. If the expectations were never shared before the marriage began, then they are surely unreasonable. Your mate is not a mind reader and should not be expected to know your deepest feelings, especially if you fail to express them. Most people have no game plan for marriage. They just let it happen to them. If it doesn't happen nicely, they may get angry enough to leave. It is important that a couple share the same vision. The Bible says, "Without a vision the people perish." This is all too true of marriages. If two people get the feeling that a relationship is going nowhere, one is just liable to bail out. James Taylor sang a haunting song called, "Another Gray Morning." It was about a person whose life had become meaningless, routine, empty, and ashamed. The person in the song decided that death was preferable to facing another gray morning. I have felt that way. The answer, however, is not suicide; it is the bringing of meaning back into our lives.

My favorite single tool to help people to reconcile after they have forgiven each other is to help them develop new and workable goals for their marriage. I am convinced that it is best not to attempt a repair of an old marriage, but rather to tear it down and build a new one. Starting over is often easier than remodeling and produces a more functional and up-to-date result. It is also more likely that the participants will come to the project as equals. If what you had before wasn't good, why try to rebuild it.

If you establish a new vision for marriage and a game plan to achieve it, it will do wonders for your attitude. I would like you to walk through the process with me so I can show you how you might apply this to your relationship. I use this method for newly-weds, remarriages, and reconciliations. It has proved to be very helpful in every case where the people did their homework. We will walk through the steps with an almost-imaginary couple. Let's call them "Paul" and "Gloria."

Paul and Gloria have two children. When they came to me they had been married ten years. Friends had talked them into coming in for help. Paul had just ended a three-month affair after hearing a Christian radio broadcast dealing with God's moral standards for husbands and wives. He seemed truly repentant and had already asked Gloria to forgive him for what he had done. She was more than willing to do that and even to admit that she had been a part of the reason that Paul had had the affair. She shared that she realized that she had let her personal appearance suffer and had become involved with church and school activities until she had no time for her husband. She actually asked him to forgive her for being a frumpy wife and promised to try hard to be better in the future. Even though I was tempted to inject that there is never an excuse for an affair, I decided that her vulnerability and openness would provide a great example for her husband, so I kept my mouth shut.

This was the first time Paul had been unfaithful, and he made a clean break from the affair. He even showed Gloria the letter that he wrote to the woman with whom he was involved and let her mail it. Gloria was satisfied that Paul was sincere in his desire to repair their relationship. So we dealt with some of the issues that were of legitimate concern to both of them. When those were resolved, I gave them an assignment. "This week I want both of you to make a list of your top ten goals for your marriage. Don't show them to each other until you get here next week. I want you to see them for the first time here."

Because the average couple has difficulty in thinking of ten areas of marriage, I always suggest a few to get them started. The areas that I gave them to consider were as follows:

1. Finances
2. Communication
3. Children
4. Extended family (any family members beyond the immediate family)
5. Recreation
6. Romance
7. Friendships
8. Spiritual goals
9. Future plans

10. Career
11. Personal goals
12. A satisfying sex life
13. Time use
14. Hobbies
15. Marriage maintenance

I further explained that they needed to turn these areas into goal statements. I suggested that if they chose to make a spiritual goal, it might be worded like "I want our marriage to bring honor to God."

Both Paul and Gloria understood the assignment, and I looked forward to seeing their goals the following week. I was not disappointed. Both did the assignment and showed a good deal of maturity in the arrangement of their priorities for marriage.

Paul's Goals	*Gloria's Goals*
1. God should be first in our marriage	1. God should be glorified in our marriage
2. We should talk every day if possible away from the children with the television off	2. I want a romantic marriage
3. We should keep the romance in our marriage	3. I hope that we can be each other's best friend
4. We should spend quality time with our children	4. I would like to spend more time with our closest friends

Paul's Goals	*Gloria's Goals*
5. We should develop a plan to get out of debt	5. I think that we need to do more things with our children
6. We should spend regular time with our relatives and friends	6. We need to plan our finances better
7. We should take vacations with each other and vacations with our children	7. I think we should improve our sex life
8. We should read books or take courses that would help us have a better marriage	8. I would like it if we planned regular time with our relatives
9. We should encourage each other to pursue a personal interest that develops our individual gifts	9. I would like regular weekend trips to get away from the children
10. We should use our spare time to enhance the quality of our family life	10. I would like it if we could buy our own home

During our session I was able to show them how many things they really had in common. They had the same basic expectations for marriage, but there were still two steps they needed to do before they were through with the assignment. I asked them to go home and blend their list into one list of ten priorities for their marriage. This would achieve two things: it would unify their vision of marriage and it would show me that they could work together in achieving their goals.

They did just fine on their assignment and ended up with this priority list:

1. We want God to be first in our marriage.
2. We want excellent communication so that we can be each other's best friend.
3. We want to have a romantic marriage.
4. We want to get out of debt so we can buy our own home.
5. We want to work at being better parents and spending more quality time together with our children.
6. We want to cultivate close family relationships and friendships that will provide a base of support for our marriage.
7. We want to encourage each other to pursue the development of individual gifts and abilities.
8. We want to have vacation times with our children and vacation times with each other.
9. We want to develop goals for our future.
10. We want to develop a family hobby that everyone will enjoy.

Their list was solid. The only thing that was missing was a plan for achieving these very realistic goals. We worked on how to do that in the office and were able to cover the first three. This is how they came out.

I.   We want God to be first in our marriage.
     A. We will attend church regularly.
     B. We will give 10 percent of our income to the Lord's work.
     C. We will join a fellowship group or Bible study to better understand the Bible and gain the support of Christian friends.
     D. We will try praying together once a day in addition to our alone time with God.
     E. We will choose a family project that involves serving the Lord. Right now we think it will be earning money for the African Children's Choir that is touring to make people aware of the homeless Ugandan children.
II. We want excellent communication so we can become each other's best friend.
     A. We will set a time each evening after dinner that we can talk for at least thirty minutes without the television on.
     B. We will not go to bed without working through an argument.
     C. We will read one book a year that helps us to better communicate.
III. We want to have a romantic marriage.
     A. We will practice new ways to express our love to each other. That will include cards and special surprises and gifts.

B. We will have one night a week in a romantic setting away from the children.
C. We will plan four weekends a year in a romantic setting without the children.
D. We will work at having times where we show affection without feeling compelled to make love.

Paul and Gloria finished their plan of action on their own, and I'm happy to report that their "almost imaginary" marriage is doing real well. They were encouraged to come in at the first sign of trouble and asked to check in every three months just to let us know how they were doing. They are doing fine.

I think I need to say that not every reconciliation goes as smoothly as did Paul and Gloria's. But when they do it's a glorious event because so much is at stake. It is certainly worth a try.

I have told you the truth about divorce in an attempt to urge you to reconcile. God help you to believe that it's possible, worth it, and the right thing to do.

Appendix A
Attitudes*

THE COLORFUL, NINETEENTH-CENTURY showman and gifted violinist Nicolo Paganini was standing before a packed house, playing through a difficult piece of music. A full orchestra surrounded him with magnificent support. Suddenly one string on his violin snapped and hung gloriously down from his instrument. Beads of perspiration popped out on his forehead. He frowned but continued to play, improvising beautifully.

To the conductor's surprise, a second string broke. And shortly thereafter, a third. Now there were three limp

---

* I am indebted to my friend and pastor, Charles R. Swindoll, for allowing me the privilege of reprinting a chapter from his wonderful book, *Strengthening Your Grip* (Waco, TX: Word, 1982). The chapter is entitled "Attitudes," and contains the best thoughts in print on this subject. This information could change the direction of your life.

strings dangling from Paganini's violin as the master performer completed the difficult composition on the one remaining string. The audience jumped to its feet and in good Italian fashion, filled the hall with shouts and screams, "Bravo! Bravo!" As the applause died down, the violinist asked the people to sit back down. Even though they knew there was no way they could expect an encore, they quietly sank back into their seats.

He held the violin high for everyone to see. He nodded at the conductor to begin the encore and then he turned back to the crowd, and with a twinkle in his eye, he smiled and shouted, "Paganini . . . and one string!" After that he placed the single-stringed Stradivarius beneath his chin and played the final piece on *one* string as the audience (and the conductor) shook their heads in silent amazement. "Paganini . . . and one string!" *And*, I might add, an attitude of fortitude.

Dr. Victor Frankl, the bold, courageous Jew who became a prisoner during the Holocaust, endured years of indignity and humiliation by the Nazis before he was finally liberated. At the beginning of his ordeal, he was marched into a gestapo courtroom. His captors had taken away his home and family, his cherished freedom, his possessions, even his watch and wedding ring. They had shaved his head and stripped his clothing off his body. There he stood before the German high command, under the glaring lights being interrogated and falsely accused. He was destitute, a helpless pawn in the hands of brutal, prejudiced, sadistic men. He had nothing. No, that isn't true. He suddenly realized there was one thing no one could ever take from him—just one. Do you know what it was?

Dr. Frankl realized he still had the power to choose his own attitude. No matter what anyone would ever do to him, regardless of what the future held for him, the attitude choice was his to make. Bitterness or forgiveness. To give up or to go on. Hatred or hope. Determination to endure or the paralysis of self-pity. It boiled down to "Frankl . . . and one string!"[1]

Words can never adequately convey the incredible impact of our attitude toward life. The longer I live the more convinced I become that life is 10 percent what happens to us and 90 percent how we respond to it.

How else can anyone explain the unbelievable feats of hurting, beat-up athletes? Take Joe Namath for instance; at age thirty he was a quarterback with sixty-five-year-old legs. Although he might have difficulty making one flight of stairs by the time he's fifty years of age, maybe before, it was attitude that kept the man in the game.

Or take Merlin Olsen and his knees. In an interview with a sports reporter, the former Los Angeles Ram all-pro defensive lineman admitted:

That year after surgery on my knee, I had to have the fluid drained weekly. Finally, the membrane got so thick they almost had to drive the needle in it with a hammer. I got to the point where I just said, ". . . get the needle in there, and get that stuff out."[2]

Joe Namath . . . Merlin Olsen . . . *and one string!*

ATTITUDES ARE ALL-IMPORTANT

This may shock you, but I believe the single most significant decision I can make on a day-to-day basis is my choice of attitude. It is more important than my past, my education, my bankroll, my successes or failures, fame or pain, what other people think of me or say about me, my circumstances, or my position. Attitude is that "single string" that keeps me going or cripples my progress. It

alone fuels my fire or assaults my hope. When my attitudes are right, there's no barrier too high, no valley
too deep, no dream too extreme, no challenge too great
for me.

Yet, we must admit that we spend more of our time
concentrating and fretting over the strings that snap,
dangle, and pop—the things that can't be changed—than
we do giving attention to the one that remains, our choice
of attitude. Stop and think about some of the things that
suck up our attention and energy, all of them inescapable
(and occasionally demoralizing).

- The tick of the clock
- The weather . . . the temperature . . . the wind!
- People's actions and reactions, *especially* the criti-
  cisms
- Who won or lost the ball game
- Delays at airports, waiting rooms, in traffic
- Results of an X-ray
- Cost of groceries, gasoline, clothes, cars—every-
  thing!
- On-the-job irritations, disappointments, workload.

The greatest waste of energy in our ecologically minded
world of the 1980s is not electricity or natural gas or any
other "product," it's the energy we waste fighting the in-
evitables! And to make matters worse, *we* are the ones
who suffer, who grow sour, who get ulcers, who become
twisted, negative and tight-fisted fighters. Some actually
die because of this.

Dozens of comprehensive studies have established this fact.
One famous study, called "Broken Heart," researched the mortality rate of 4,500 widowers within six months of their wives'
deaths. Compared with other men the same age, the widowers
had a mortality rate 40 percent higher.[3]

Major F. J. Harold Kushner, an army medical officer held by the Viet Cong for over five years, cites an example of death because of an attitudinal failure. In a fascinating article in *New York* magazine this tragic yet true account is included:

> Among the prisoners in Kushner's POW camp was a tough young marine, 24 years old, who had already survived two years of prison-camp life in relatively good health. Part of the reason for this was that the camp commander had promised to release the man if he cooperated. Since this had been done before with others, the marine turned into a model POW and the leader of the camp's thought-reform group. As time passed he gradually realized that his captors had lied to him. When the full realization of this took hold he became a zombie. He refused to do all work, rejected all offers of food and encouragement, and simply lay on his cot sucking his thumb. In a matter of weeks he was dead.[4]

Caught in the vice grip of lost hope, life became too much for the once-tough marine to handle. When that last string snapped, there was nothing left.

THE VALUE OF ATTITUDES: SCRIPTURE SPEAKS

In the little letter Paul wrote to the Christians in Philippi, he didn't mince words when it came to attitudes. Although a fairly peaceful and happy flock, the Philippians had a few personality skirmishes that could have derailed them and hindered their momentum. Knowing how counterproductive that would be, he came right to the point: their attitudes.

If therefore there is any encouragement in Christ, if there is any consolation of love, if there is any fellowship of the Spirit, if any affection and compassion, make my joy complete by being of the same mind, maintaining the same love, united in spirit, intent on one purpose (Phil. 2:1-2).

What does all this mean? Well, let's go back and take a look. There *is* encouragement in the Person of Christ. There *is* love. There is also plenty of "fellowship of the Spirit" for the Christian to enjoy. Likewise, affection and compassion. Heaven is full and running over with these things even though earth is pretty barren at times. So Paul pleads for us to tap into that positive, encouraging storehouse. How? By "being of the same mind." He's telling us to take charge of our own minds; clearly a command. We Christians have the God-given ability to put our minds on those things that build up, strengthen, encourage, and help ourselves and others. "Do that!" commands the Lord.

Attitude of Unselfish Humility

Paul gets specific at verses 3 and 4 of Philippians 2:

Do nothing from selfishness or empty conceit, but with humility of mind let each of you regard one another as more important than himself; do not merely look out for your own personal interests, but also for the interests of others.

This is a mental choice we make, a decision not to focus on self . . . me . . . my . . . mine, but on the other person. It's a servant mentality the Scriptures are encouraging. I have written an entire book[5] on this subject, so I'll not elaborate here except to say that few virtues are more needed today. When we strengthen our grip on attitudes, a great place to begin is with humility —authentic and gracious unselfishness.

Our example? Read on:

Have this attitude in yourselves which was also in Christ Jesus, who, although He existed in the form of God, did not regard equality with God a thing to be grasped, but emptied

Himself, taking the form of a bond-servant, and being made in the likeness of men.

And being found in appearance as a man, He humbled Himself by becoming obedient to the point of death, even death on a cross (Phil. 2:5–8).

Maybe you have never stopped to think about it, but behind the scenes, it was an attitude that brought the Savior down to us. He deliberately chose to come among us because He realized and valued our need. He placed a higher significance on it than His own comfort and prestigious position. In humility, He set aside the glory of heaven and came to be among us. He refused to let His position keep us at arm's length.

Attitude of Positive Encouragement

Listen to another verse in the same chapter: "Do all things without grumbling or disputing" (v. 14).

Ouch! If ever a generation needed that counsel, *ours* does! It is virtually impossible to complete a day without falling into the trap of "grumbling or disputing." It is so easy to pick up the habit of negative thinking. Why? Because there are so many things around us that prompt us to be irritable. Let's not kid ourselves, life is *not* a bed of roses!

On my last birthday my sister Luci gave me a large scroll-like poster. Since our humor is somewhat similar, she knew I'd get a kick out of the stuff printed on it. She suggested I tack it up on the back of my bathroom door so I could review it regularly. It's a long list of some of the inescapable "laws" of life that can make us irritable "grumblers and disputers" if we let them. They are commonly called "Murphy's Laws." Here's a sample:

- Nothing is as easy as it looks; everything takes longer than you think; if anything can go wrong it will.
- Murphy was an optimist.

- A day without a crisis is a total loss.
- The other line always moves faster.
- The chance of the bread falling with the peanut butter-and-jelly side down is directly proportional to the cost of the carpet.
- Inside every large problem is a series of small problems struggling to get out.
- 90% of everything is crud.
- Whatever hits the fan will not be evenly distributed.
- No matter how long or hard you shop for an item, after you've bought it, it will be on sale somewhere cheaper.
- Any tool dropped while repairing a car will roll underneath to the exact center.
- The repairman will never have seen a model quite like yours before.
- You will remember that you forgot to take out the trash when the garbage truck is two doors away.
- Friends come and go, but enemies accumulate.
- The light at the end of the tunnel is the headlamp of an oncoming train.
- Beauty is only skin deep, but ugly goes clear to the bone.[6]

Every item on the list is an attitude assailant! And the simple fact is they are so true, we don't even have to imagine their possibility—*they happen*. I have a sneaking suspicion they happened in Paul's day too. So when he writes about grumbling and disputing, he wasn't coming from an ivory tower. A positive, encouraging attitude is essential for survival in a world saturated with Murphy's Laws.

Attitude of Genuine Joy

Joy is really the underlying theme of Philippians—joy that isn't fickle, needing a lot of "things" to keep it smiling . . . joy that is deep and consistent—the oil that reduces the friction of life.

Finally, my brethren, rejoice in the Lord (Phil. 3:1a).

Therefore, my beloved brethren whom I long to see, my joy and crown, so stand firm in the Lord, my beloved. . . . Rejoice in the Lord always; again I will say, rejoice! Let your forbearing spirit be known to all men. The Lord is near. Be anxious for nothing, but in everything by prayer and supplication with thanksgiving let your requests be made known to God. And the peace of God, which surpasses all comprehension, shall guard your hearts and your minds in Christ Jesus (Phil. 4:1, 4–7).

There it is again—*the mind.* Our minds can be kept free of anxiety (those strings that snap) as we dump the load of our cares on the Lord in prayer. By getting rid of the stuff that drags us down, we create space for the joy to take its place.

Think of it like this: Circumstances occur that could easily crush us. They may originate on the job or at home or even during the weekend when we are relaxing. Unexpectedly, they come. Immediately we have a choice to make . . . an attitude choice. We can hand the circumstance to God and ask Him to take control or we can roll up our mental sleeves and slug it out. Joy awaits our decision. If we do as Philippians 4:6–7 suggests, peace replaces panic and joy moves into action. It is ready, but it is not pushy.

AGGRESSIVE-PASSIVE ALTERNATIVES

Let's not kid ourselves. When we deliberately choose not to stay positive and deny joy a place in our lives, we'll usually gravitate in one of two directions, sometimes both—the direction of blame or self-pity.

Blame

The aggressive attitude reacts to circumstances with blame. We blame ourselves or someone else, or God, or if we can't find a tangible scapegoat, we blame "fate." What an absolute waste! When we blame ourselves, we multiply our guilt, we rivet ourselves to the past (another "dangling" unchangeable), and we decrease our already low self-esteem. If we choose to blame God, we cut off our single source of power. Doubt replaces trust, and we put down roots of bitterness that can make us cynical. If we blame others, we enlarge the distance between us and them. We alienate. We poison a relationship. We settle for something much less than God ever intended. And on top of all that, we do not find relief!

Blame never affirms, it assaults.
Blame never restores, it wounds.
Blame never solves, it complicates.
Blame never unites, it separates.
Blame never smiles, it frowns.
Blame never forgives, it rejects.
Blame never forgets, it remembers.
Blame never builds, it destroys.

Let's admit it—not until we stop blaming will we start enjoying health and happiness again! This was underscored as I read the following words recently:

. . . one of the most innovative psychologists in this half of the twentieth century . . . said recently that he considers only one kind of counselee relatively hopeless: that person who blames other people for his or her problems. If you can own the mess you're in, he says, there is hope for you and help available. As long as you blame others, you will be a victim for the rest of your life.[7]

Self-Pity

The passive attitude responds to circumstances in an opposite manner, feeling sorry for oneself. I find this just as damaging as blaming, sometimes more so. In fact, I'm ready to believe that self-pity is "Private Enemy No. 1." Things turn against us, making us recipients of unfair treatment, like innocent victims of a nuclear mishap. We neither expect it nor deserve it, and to make matters worse, it happens at the worst possible time. We're too hurt to blame.

Our natural tendency is to curl up in the fetal position and sing the silly little children's song:

> Nobody loves me, everybody hates me,
> I think I'll eat some worms.

Which helps nobody. But what else can we do when the bottom drops out? Forgive me if this sounds too simplistic, but the only thing worth doing is usually the last thing we try doing—turning it over to our God, the Specialist, who has never yet been handed an impossibility He couldn't handle. Grab that problem by the throat and thrust it skyward!

There is a familiar story in the New Testament that always makes me smile. Paul and his traveling companion Silas had been beaten and dumped in a dungeon. It was *so* unfair! But this mistreatment did not steal their joy or dampen their confidence in God. Their circumstance, however, could not have been more bleak. They were there to stay.

But about midnight Paul and Silas were praying and singing hymns of praise to God, and the prisoners were listening to them (Acts 16:25).

I would imagine! The sounds of confident praying and joyful singing are not usually heard from a stone prison. But Paul and Silas had determined they would not be paralyzed by self-pity. And as they prayed and sang, the unbelievable transpired.

And suddenly there came a great earthquake, so that the foundations of the prisonhouse were shaken; and immediately all the doors were opened, and everyone's chains were unfastened.
And when the jailer had been roused out of sleep and had seen the prison doors opened, he drew his sword and was about to kill himself, supposing that the prisoners had escaped.
But Paul cried out with a loud voice, saying, "Do yourself no harm, for we are all here!" (vv. 26–28).

With calm reassurance, Paul spoke words of encouragement to the jailer. He even promised there would be no attempt to escape. And if you take the time to read the full account (vv. 29–40) you will find how beautifully God used their attitude to change the entire face of their situation. I love such stories! They stand as monumental reminders that the right attitude choice can literally transform our circumstance, no matter how black and hopeless it may appear. And best of all, the right attitude becomes contagious!
I was sharing some of these thoughts at a large gathering in Chicago not long ago. It was Founders' Week at Moody Bible Institute, the annual time of celebration when Christians from all over the United States come to the school for a week of Bible teaching, singing, and interaction together. Following one of my talks, a lady I never met wrote me this letter.

Dear Chuck,

I want you to know I've been here all week and I've enjoyed every one of your talks. I know they will help me in my remaining years. . . .

I love your sense of humor. Humor has done a lot to help me in my spiritual life. How could I have raised 12 children starting at age 32 and not have had a sense of humor! I married at age 31. I didn't worry about getting married, I just left my future to God's will. But every night I hung a pair of men's pants on the bed and knelt down and prayed:

> "Father in heaven, hear my prayer
> And grant it if you can,
> I've hung a pair of trousers here,
> Please fill them with a man!"

I had a good laugh. In fact, I thought it was such a classic illustration of the right mental attitude toward life that I read it to my congregation in Fullerton, California, when I returned. Mom and a sick daughter were home, but dad and an older son in his twenties were present and heard me read the letter. The mother (who knew nothing of the letter) wrote me a note a couple weeks later. She was brief and to the point. She was concerned about her older son. She said that for the last week or so he had been sleeping in his bed with a bikini draped over the footboard. She wanted to know if I might know why . . . or if this was something she needed to worry about.

FOOD FOR THE RIGHT ATTITUDE

Since our choice of attitude is so important, our minds need fuel to feed on. Philippians 4:8 gives us a good place to start:

Finally, brethren, whatever is true, whatever is honorable, whatever is right, whatever is pure, whatever is lovely, whatever is of good repute, if there is any excellence and if anything worthy of praise, let your mind dwell on these things.

Good advice: "Let your mind *dwell* on these things." Fix your attention on these six specifics in life. Not unreal far-fetched dreams, but things that are *true*, real, valid. Not cheap, flippant, superficial stuff, but things that are *honorable;* i.e., worthy of respect. Not things that are wrong and unjust, critical and negative, but that which is *right*. Not thoughts that are carnal, smutty, and obscene, but that which is *pure* and wholesome. Not things that prompt arguments and defense in others, but those that are *lovely,* agreeable, attractive, winsome. Finally, not slander, gossip, and put-downs, but information of *good report,* the kind that builds up and causes grace to flow.

Do you do this? Is this the food you serve your mind? We are back where we started, aren't we? The choice is yours. The other discouraging strings on your instrument may snap and hang loosely—no longer available or useful, but nobody can *make* you a certain way. That is strictly up to you.

And may I take the liberty to say something very directly? Some of you who read these words are causing tremendous problems because of your attitude. You are capable. You are intelligent. You are qualified and maybe even respected for your competence. But your attitude is taking a toll on those who are near you—those you live with, those you work with, those you touch in life. For some of you, your home is a battleground, a mixture of negativism, sarcasm, pressure, cutting comments, and blame. For others, you have allowed self-pity to move in under your roof and you have foolishly surrendered mental territory that once was healthy and happy. You are laughing less and complaining more. You have to admit that the "one string" on which you can play—if you choose to do so—is out of tune.

As your friend, let me urge you to take charge of your mind and emotions today. Let your mind feast on nutritious food for a change. Refuse to grumble and criticize! Reject those alien thoughts that make you a petty, bitter person. Play that single string once again! Let it yield a sweet, winsome melody that this old world needs so desperately. Yes, you *can* if you *will.*

I was sitting at the Christian Bookseller's Association final banquet the last evening of the convention in 1981. My mind was buzzing as I was arranging my thoughts for the speech. I was a bit nervous and my attitude was somewhere between blame ("Why in the world did you say 'yes,' Swindoll?") and self-pity ("There are a dozen or more people who could do a lot better job than you, dummy!") when the spotlight turned from the head table to a young woman sitting in a wheelchair off to the side. She was to sing that evening.

I was greatly encouraged to see her. I was strengthened in my spirit as I thought back over Joni Eareckson's pilgrimage since 1967—broken neck; loss of feeling from her shoulders down; numerous operations; broken romance; the death of dreams; no more swimming, horseback riding, skating, running, dancing; not even an evening stroll, ever again. All those strings now dangled from her life. But there sat a radiant, remarkable, rare woman who had chosen not to quit.

I shall never forget the song she sang that quieted my nerves and put things in perspective:

> When peace, like a river, attendeth my way,
> When sorrows like sea billows roll;
> Whatever my lot, Thou hast taught me to say,
> "It is well, it is well with my soul."

> Though Satan should buffet, tho' trials should come,
> Let this blest assurance control,
> That Christ has regarded my helpless estate,
> And hath shed His own blood for my soul.[8]

Do you know what all of us witnessed that evening? More than a melody. More than grand and glorious lyrics. Much, much more. In a very real sense, we witnessed the surpassing value of an attitude in a life that literally had nothing else to cling to. Joni Eareckson . . . and one string.

DISCUSSION QUESTIONS AND SUGGESTIONS TO HELP YOU STRENGTHEN YOUR GRIP ON ATTITUDES

• Let's begin by describing or defining *attitude*. What is it? How does it differ from things like conduct and competence? Since it *is* different from both, does one's attitude affect either one? Explain your answer.

• Biblically, we found that God says a lot about our attitudes in His Book. Can you recall one or two passages in particular that took on new meaning as a result of this booklet? Try to be specific as you state the practical significance of the scriptural reference.

• Because Philippians 4:8 was a scriptural climax to the booklet, let's zero in on the six areas the verse instructs us to "let your mind dwell on." Taking each, one at a time, work your way along. Stop, think, meditate, and then talk about how each fits into some category of your life that has begun to trouble you or perhaps challenge you.

• Now let's talk about some of the darker sides of our attitudes. Risk being deeply honest as you open up and admit the battleground within. In which area(s) do you face your greatest struggles? For example, are you more often negative than positive? Or are you stubborn and closed rather than open and willing to hear? How's your attitude toward people *very* different from you? Are you prejudiced? Look over James 2:1–4.

• Compare a few verses from the book of Proverbs. Like Proverbs 4:20–23; 12:25; 15:13, 15, 30. Choose one and explain how it applies to your own personal life.

• And now—let's pray. For a change, don't pray for yourself, but for the person sitting on your left. Call his or her name before the Lord and ask for one or two specifics on that person's behalf. Give Him thanks for the changes He will bring in your attitude and the attitudes of others. As they happen this week in your life, note the changes and give God praise in your heart.

NOTES

[1] Dale E. Galloway, *Dream a New Dream* (Wheaton, IL: Tyndale House Publishers, 1975), p. 59.

[2] Mark Kram, "The Face of Pain," *Sports Illustrated*, 44, no. 10 (March 8, 1976): 60.

[3] Philip Yancey, *Where Is God When It Hurts* (Grand Rapids: Zondervan Publishing House, 1978), p. 142.

[4] Douglas Colligan, "That Helpless Feeling: The Dangers of Stress," *New York*, July 14, 1975, p. 28.

[5] Charles R. Swindoll, *Improving Your Serve* (Waco, TX: Word Books Publisher, 1981).

[6] "Murphy's Law" (231 Adrian Road, Millbrae, CA: Celestial Arts, 1979).

[7] Bruce Larson, *There's a Lot More to Health Than Not Being Sick* (Waco, TX: Word Books Publisher, 1981), p. 46.

[8] Horatio G. Spafford, "It Is Well with My Soul," copyright 1918 The John Church Co. Used by permission of the publisher.

Appendix B
Good Counsel*

ANGIE *had desired nothing more in life than to be a submissive Christian wife and loving mother. But the reality of spending her days cooped up with three small children while her husband, Ron, drifted from one low-paying job to another did not match her dreams. When Ron finally landed a good job as a foreman at a machinery manufacturing company, only to lose it after a dispute with his boss, Angie's hope began to wane. Their savings dwindling, she started lashing out at Ron. During one shouting match, Angie said, "I can't take it anymore. Either we get help or I'm leaving!"*

---

* I am indebted to Kelsey Menehan for allowing me to share with you her most excellent article on choosing an effective counselor: "Good Counsel," *Today's Christian Woman* (May-June 1986): 48–53, 75. It is a thoughtful and well-written article.

MARY *cried off and on for hours when her youngest son left for college in another state. For mornings afterward she could barely lift her head from the pillow. She moved through her days in slow motion, scarcely able to make simple decisions like what to wear or what to fix for dinner. The Bible, whose words had never failed to comfort her before, now seemed dull and wooden. When Mary hadn't snapped out of her "blue funk" in two months, her husband voiced his concern. "Nothing I say seems to help," he said. "Go talk to somebody, okay?"*

SHEILA *was a sophomore at a Christian college when she began having terrifying, sexually violent dreams in which she was the unwilling victim. During her waking hours Sheila felt anxious and would often pray, "Lord, make these feelings go away! Please!" But the sense of impending doom persisted. Finally, Sheila worked up the courage to tell a trusted friend about the dreams. Her friend looked shocked. "Please, Sheila, for your sake, go to a counselor," her friend pleaded. "I'll pay for it."*

M AN IS BORN TO TROUBLE as surely as sparks fly up- ward," Eliphaz told the much-afflicted Job, and it seems neither people nor sparks have changed their behavior much since then. Trouble is part of what it means to be human in a fallen world. People die and those left behind grieve. Children rebel. Spouses grow apart. Friends feud. Employees get fired. Businesses fail. Self-esteem sags. Dreams die. God seems distant.

"The journey through life is a series of crises," writes Norman Wright in *Crisis Counseling* (Here's Life), "some of which are predictable and expected and some of which are total surprises." Yet most of the time we manage to negotiate life's course fairly well, even when there

are bumps or potholes or sudden detours. We pray for
strength and it comes—often inexplicably. We turn to
our extended family and receive consolation and wise
advice. Christian friends listen and tell us we are loved.

We cope. Sometimes we even triumph.

But as Angie and Mary and Sheila discovered, some
potholes on life's road seem to grow into chasms right
before our eyes. "I kept thinking that things would get
better, but they didn't," Angie confessed. On these occasions prayer, regular church attendance, daily devotions,
and the support of family and friends *alone* may not be
enough to bridge the gap.

An heretical thought? Some would think so. After all,
Christ is the answer, we have always been taught. *We can
do all things through Christ who strengthens us.*

Yet sometimes we cannot do "all things" in isolation.
We need someone to stand with us at the edge of the
chasm—a bridge builder, if you will.

When Angie, Mary, and Sheila reached the edge, they
found the extra guidance they needed from trained
"people helpers."

Angie and her husband consulted with their pastor, a
skilled counselor, and over a period of weeks learned
better ways of handling their anger while working to
overcome feelings of low self-esteem. "I don't think we
could have made it without his help," Angie says of the
sessions.

Mary learned that she was not alone in her reaction to
the empty nest. During several months of counseling with
a trained social worker, she began to find new meaning
for her life beyond the roles of mother and nurturer.

Working with a psychiatrist, Sheila uncovered memories from an abusive childhood that were thwarting her
emotional and spiritual growth. As she worked through

layer upon layer of anger and pain, Sheila found the courage to forgive and move on.

In recent years, thousands of Christians with problems ranging from confusion about career choice to suicidal fantasies have found the courage to move on with the help of a variety of people helpers. These helpers go by many names: marriage and family counselors, social workers, psychotherapists, biblical counselors, psychiatrists, pastoral counselors, spiritual directors, clinical psychologists.

But just who are these people helpers? How can they help me with my problems? How can I find the right one for myself or someone I love? And how do I know I need a counselor in the first place? These are some of the questions Christian women ask when a problem is threatening to overwhelm them. And they are wise to ask, because while counseling has been practiced in various forms since ancient times (the Bible contains many references to receiving "counsel"), as a profession it is a relatively new and very complex field.

Scientific psychology, the study of both human and animal behavior, was born about one hundred years ago and has since spawned a baffling array of theories which are used in various ways by counselors. Years ago some of these theories concluded that religious belief was a neurosis to be cured, not an integral part of a person's wholeness. Christians with severe problems who sought help from secular psychologists were fortunate if they emerged from counseling with their faith intact. Yet pastors and lay Christians often felt ill-equipped to help these people.

Understandably, for many years Christians tended to view any integration of biblical faith with psychological theory as spiritual suicide. But today, a growing number of Christians are studying these theories and are separating the "wheat" from the "chaff." These "Christian counselors" believe that psychological findings, tested against biblical truth, can contribute to the understanding and solution of problems. "The Word of God . . . was not meant to be God's sole revelation about people-helping," writes professor and counselor Gary Collins in his book *Christian Counseling: A Comprehensive Guide* (Word). "In medicine, teaching, and other 'people-centered' helping fields, mankind has been permitted to learn much about God's creation through science and academic study. Why, then, should psychology be singled out as the one field that has nothing to contribute to the work of the counselor?"

David Seamands, a counselor and professor at Asbury College, sees a definite trend toward the successful integration of psychology and the Christian faith. "Thirty years ago, pastors used to preach against me," he says. "Now a lot more Christian people are getting the counseling help they need. They're not afraid to seek it or to pay for it."

This is welcome news for hurting Christians who want help but are reluctant to seek it from a secular counselor who does not share their Christian beliefs. Today in most cities and towns one can find Christians trained in counseling. In addition, some larger churches have opened counseling centers where people can get help from trained professionals and lay counselors.

Taking the First Step

Even so, for many Christians that first step—actually making an appointment with a people helper—is fraught with anxiety. Women are more likely than men to seek help, but, as Paul G. Quinnett writes in *The Troubled People Book* (Continuum), "the fairer sex is no less proud or

less motivated to take care of things without assistance."
No one wants to admit she has a problem that requires
outside help, and the believer faces the additional stigma
that says, "The Lord should be enough. Prayer should
work. Why do I still have problems? What kind of Christian am I anyway?"

"Many Christians can't understand why they can't pray
away their problems," says André Bustanoby, a counselor
in the Washington, D.C., area. "They have an inadequate
view of the doctrine of man. They equate humanness
with the sin nature. The two are not the same. Our task is
not to flee from our humanity, but to understand that we
are twice-born people with twofold needs."

William Diehm, a clinical psychologist in California,
says some Christians actually feel they would be disloyal
to their faith if they sought counseling. After all, isn't
Christ their counselor? To these people Diehm suggests:
"Learn to consider a counselor as a special type of
preacher who ministers to the needs of one person instead of to an audience."

What kind of problems require outside intervention?
Generally, counselors agree, a problem is whatever a person defines as one. "What may be a problem to one person
may be an annoyance to another," says Mary Franzen
Clark, a therapist in Livonia, Michigan. Seamands de-
scribes problems that require counseling as "any repeti-
tive pattern of personal or spiritual defeat that the regular
arenas of grace—prayer, church, support group—seem
unable to help." The following symptoms may be clues
that help is needed: loss of joy; apathy; uncontrolled crying jags; feeling out of control; inability to make simple
decisions; belief that others are out to get you; ordinary
behavior gone out of control, such as eating, drinking,
cleaning rituals; difficulty dealing with a loss or a change;
disruption of family or social relationships; a close friend

or family member's suggestion that counseling might be beneficial.

Sheila, from the opening stories, sought help after several friends encouraged her to. "I thought I was a very well-adjusted person, yet all these people kept telling me to get help. I couldn't figure it out. So I went to a therapist." She's glad she did.

But with such an array of counselors and specialists to choose from, how does one find a good counselor? It's not easy, but several counselors we surveyed suggested these steps:

Get referrals from people you trust. Ask your pastor or a Christian physician for names of competent counselors. Talk to friends who have been in counseling. From whom have they gotten the best help? If you live in a small community, a guidance counselor in the local school system may have professional contacts to whom he or she can refer you. The Narramore Christian Foundation and the Christian Association of Psychological Studies (CAPS) will also make referrals.

Check out a counselor's credentials. "Counselors who describe themselves as Christian counselors have sprung up like mushrooms, or perhaps I should say toadstools," says Seamands. "Not all are trained or competent." So it is important to find out if he or she has the appropriate degrees and is licensed by the state. The credentials required vary among the different kinds of people helpers.

If you are seeking help from a lay counselor at a church, be sure to inquire about his or her training and supervision. And check the credentials of the counseling program's director.

Ask that the first session be a consultation. A consultation, writes Quinnett, does not imply a commitment beyond the first visit. You pay for one session, discuss your problems, and decide with the counselor if therapy should be undertaken.

During this initial session both you and the counselor will be sizing each other up. You should be looking for several important qualities in the counselor. A four-year-study conducted with hospital patients and a variety of counselors revealed that patients improved when their therapist showed high levels of warmth, genuineness, and empathy.

Warmth implies "caring, respecting, possessing a sincere, non-smothering concern for the counselee regardless of his or her action or attitudes," writes Collins. *Genuineness* means the counselor avoids phoniness or playing a superior role. "They are real people who themselves are on the edge of growth, offering themselves as living examples of struggle and growth in the Christian life," says Bustanoby. *Empathy,* he continues, means "entering a client's world of pain and accurately touching where they hurt—yet in a nonjudgmental way, much as Jesus did with the woman caught in adultery."

What all of these qualities add up to is love; the counselor should be loving. Love is "incomparably the greatest psychotherapeutic agent . . . something that professional psychiatry cannot of itself create, focus, or release," said Gordon Allport, former president of the American Psychological Association.

Christian counselors, of course, are not the only ones who can demonstrate love, but Collins suggests that since Christianity ideally offers a life based on love, Christian helpers may succeed where secular counseling fails.

These qualities of a counselor may be difficult to pinpoint in one session, especially when you're both nervous. One rule of thumb, says Quinnett: "If you go away

feeling demeaned, belittled, or like a naughty child, and
the thought of making another appointment sticks in your
throat, don't make it."

During the first session, you will also want to clarify
what the counseling is all about. The therapist should
describe how therapy works, how many sessions may be
required, who else may be asked to come in (spouse, children, and so forth), what his or her style of therapy is,
how he or she will pursue helping you, and how much it
will cost. You should feel free to express your needs and
negotiate. For example, your budget may not allow for
the frequency of sessions the counselor suggests. Discuss
all financial ramifications up front and in detail. (Counseling can cost as much as one hundred dollars per session, although some people helpers use a sliding scale
based on your income in setting fees.) If you decide to
continue in therapy with this counselor, you also will
want to make clear where the bills are sent, whether or
not your insurance pays, whether or not your boss may
know that you're in counseling, and so forth.

The goal of the first session is to test the waters, to see
if an atmosphere of trust can be established. "The patient
is in a vulnerable position, spilling her guts to someone
she doesn't know, speaking the unspeakable," says Clark.
"If there is no trust, then the communication will be lim-
ited and so will the therapy."

If you're uncomfortable after one, or at the most two,
sessions, and sense that rapport or trust is not develop-
ing, look for another counselor.

Let the Buyer Beware

When you're hurting, it's natural to want to latch on
to someone who seems willing to listen and empathize.
But as any consumer of a service, you are wise to be

discriminating. There are wolves among the sheep. Here are some clues for spotting them.

Leaving faith at the door. Mary Vander Goot, a counselor in Michigan, warns: "Be wary of any counselor who cannot answer yes to the question, 'Do you recognize that religious faith is a constructive influence in the lives of most believers?'" Although many nonChristian counselors today demonstrate respect for a person's faith (even if they don't share it), there are still those who downplay the importance of belief.

And surprisingly, there are some Christian counselors who do the same, leaving little room for prayer or Christian theology in the counseling session. "I'm amazed at the number of 'Christian' counselors who leave Christianity at the door," says Collins. Ideally, you should find a counselor who is a genuine Christian with beliefs similar to yours, not just a churchgoer, says Seamands. "If you can't find an evangelical," he continues, "at least find someone who is sympathetic to the faith and is not in any way antimoral or amoral."

Simplistic approaches. On the other end of the spectrum, some counselors have expressed concern about certain confrontational forms of "biblical counseling" which reject all insights from the fields of psychology and psychiatry. Proponents of this form of counseling believe that people's problems stem from only three sources—physical disorders, individual sin, or the Devil. The pastor—the only person competent to counsel—must confront the counselee verbally with her or his sin using the Word as the only source.

Such an approach may be helpful to some who are committing blatant sins and have a tendency to transfer blame to others, but it can be harmful to those with other kinds of problems. "I get hundreds of calls and from people, many of them women, who say, 'I went to a counselor and all he did was preach at me. He didn't help me at all'," Seamands says. "Some people are horrible victims of other people's sin, through no fault or choice of their own." This style of counseling, he adds, is "absurd" for treating most cases of depression.

A good model for how to counsel is Jesus Christ, writes Collins. "Jesus used a variety of counseling techniques, depending on the situation, the nature of the counselee, and the specific problem. At times he listened to people carefully, without giving much direction, but on other occasions he taught decisively. He encouraged and supported but also confronted and challenged."

Sexual malpractice. Sadly, some counselors, even some Christian ones, use the therapeutic relationship as an opportunity to engage in illicit sex. A woman should be wary if a male counselor acts overly friendly physically, suggests that they meet at odd times or places, or makes overtures that are in any way suggestive.

"If a woman ever feels uncomfortable sexually," says Clark, "she should raise the issue or ask to see someone else."

"I'm wrong even when I'm right." More women than men seek counseling when they're experiencing difficulties in coping with life. And most counselors show great respect for women who muster up the courage to seek help. But some counselors, even some Christian ones, tend to label women with problems as "hysterical," "overreacting," "weak," or "inferior." These are sexist attitudes, but women often do not recognize them as such. Counseling only reinforces their already low opinion of themselves. The problem is compounded by the fact that until recently the study of psychology has focused on male, not female, development.

It may be difficult to come right out and ask a male counselor about his attitudes toward women, but be alert to statements such as "Well, most women are like that" or "I don't think your perceptions are valid" or "You're being overly emotional" that might betray his thought patterns.

Getting the Most from Counseling

You've taken the courageous step of admitting you have a problem and you are seeking help. Now what can you do to make the process a profitable one?

If possible, set a goal. What do you want from counseling? Your answer may be as clear as "I want to be able to fly in an airplane" or "I want to be able to ask my boss for a raise." Or it might be somewhat more vague: "I want to be happier" or "I want to feel more in control of my life." The best goals are simple and clear, but even a nebulous goal gives you and your counselor something toward which you can work together. Goals may change as you learn more about what's bothering you. Sometimes the very struggle to clarify goals becomes the focus of the counseling relationship as you discover for yourself what you most want in life.

Don't expect a quick fix. Instant miracles, instant answers, immediate responses to acts of faith—this approach to problems has crept into our attitudes, aided and abetted by TV preachers. This "expect a miracle" mentality, says Clark, "leaves the person with a longer-term spiritual struggle, feeling betrayed by God. There's great danger in suggesting that someone can overcome depression in two weeks. It sets people up for failure and the psychological consequences can be severe." Real growth takes time, sometimes lots of it.

Be open. "When I went to a counselor for the first

time, I was frightened and curious," Sheila says, "so I tried to outwit the therapist. I thought because I was bright and articulate I could cover up what was wrong." Sheila's defenses eventually were broken down by a skillful counselor, and Sheila began to see that being as open as possible worked to her advantage.

This is not to say it's easy. Women in particular have been socialized to put their best foot forward, to win affection, to make a good impression. But a counselor is not a friend to be won over; he or she is a professional hired to help you.

A counselor can help you only if he or she knows the good *and* the bad about you and your situation. So let your hair down and be encouraged by the fact that your counselor has probably heard it all before. Indeed, "there are no new things under the sun."

Find a support group. Many women don't want to tell anyone—let alone someone whose respect they cherish—that they're receiving counseling. But you most need warm acceptance and support while you're struggling to get a handle on your problems. "Find at least one friend who will listen to your trials in the process," says Kaye Cook, a counselor and professor at Gordon College. "It can be long and frustrating."

Supportive friends will also help you keep a perspective on your problems. "It's easy to trick yourself into thinking that because you're seeing a therapist you don't have to be nice to people," says Sheila. "It gives you an excuse not to get on with life." Friends can steer you away from excessive self-absorption and a "woe is me" attitude.

Pray continually. Many Christian counselors will pray with you before or during your counseling sessions. But don't suppose that God's activity in your life ends after one hour. Keep praying—for insight, clarity, healing—as you go about your daily activities. "I consider a counselor a temporary assistant of the Holy Spirit," Seamands says. "The goal of therapy is to get the counselee to the place where she can go directly to God through prayer. The ultimate therapy is prayer. There will be times when it seems like no progress is being made. It's like rowing around an island. You row and pray, row and pray, waiting for a place to land."

Finding those places to land—those insights and clues that will bring understanding and finally healing—is the goal of counseling. The process of discovering truth about yourself and about God, truth that will ultimately set you free, may feel at times like pulling an oar through molasses. So while you "row and pray" it's important to remember that an unseen Counselor is in the boat, pointing your way to shore.